DOLLS' HOUSE
inspirations

DOLLS' HOUSE

inspirations

Jean Nisbett

Alec Nisbett, Photographer

GUILD OF MASTER CRAFTSMAN
PUBLICATIONS

This book is for Amber, Jay, Amy and Thomas

First published 2007 by
Guild of Master Craftsman Publications Ltd,
166 High Street, Lewes,
East Sussex BN7 1XU

Text © Jean Nisbett, 2007
Photographs © Alec Nisbett, 2007
Copyright in the Work © Guild of Master
Craftsman Publications Ltd, 2007

ISBN 978-1-86108-509-2

A catalogue record of this book is available
from the British Library.

Production Manager: Jim Bulley
Managing Editor: Gerrie Purcell
Project Editor: Rachel Netherwood
Photography: Alec Nisbett
Managing Art Editor: Gilda Pacitti
Design: Chloë Alexander

Typefaces: Monotype Goudy & ITC Goudy Sans
Colour origination: Altaimage
Printed and bound: Sino Publishing

Imperial and metric
The standard dolls' house scale is 1/12, which was
based originally on imperial measures: one inch
represents one foot. Although many craftspeople
use metric measurements, dolls' house hobbyists
in Britian and especially America still use feet
and inches. In this book imperial measures are
given first, followed by their metric equivalent,
which may be rounded up or down a little. Most
of the miniatures in this book are to 1/12 scale.

Contents

Introduction

Today's dolls' house hobby is international; from Sweden to Hong Kong and from Spain to Australia, hobbyists interchange ideas through dolls' house magazines and websites.

Dolls' houses and miniature furniture can be seen and bought globally; makers exhibit at miniatures fairs in many countries and many have websites so that you can access and order just the house or special piece of furniture that you need.

When my first book, *The Complete Dolls' House Book* was published in 1993, things were very different. It was intended as a complete guide to the hobby as practised at that time, with information about the dolls' houses that were available and how to achieve period decoration in 1:12 scale. That book showed examples of superlative dolls' houses and furniture made by leading miniaturists and offered a wealth of ideas to take less expensive houses through to completion. At the time the materials available were limited, and not always easy to source, and houses to assemble from kits could be mentioned only briefly.

❶ This pretty Georgian dolls' house shop has given me endless pleasure over the years; I change the window displays frequently to give it a fresh look.

❷ Bay windows provide additional space to show off special furniture or arrange a little scene.

Since then, building a dolls' house from a kit has become as popular as buying one ready-made, and for many hobbyists this is a rewarding and economical way to achieve the house of their dreams. And this not only applies to houses, but furniture too. Today's miniaturists are ready to tackle a wider range of projects than ever before.

This book reflects these advances and is addressed to hobbyists who have many different interests and objectives. It caters for the collector who wants a fully finished dolls' house in which to display their professionally made furniture. It offers advice to those who want a ready-made house to decorate in their own way and gives step-by-step instructions to those who want to assemble one from a kit and then also make some of the furniture.

I have selected a wide range of styles so that whatever kind of dolls' house you choose you will find a similar example to follow. Each project is covered in detail, with advice on construction, decoration and how to make your own dolls' house look its very best.

Furniture made by professional miniaturists is shown in close-up and in room settings. In addition, there are furniture kits to assemble that will suit each chosen period; furniture to paint or refinish, and for a modern dolls' house, simple furniture to make at little or no expense. The miniaturist gardener is not left out: a selection of garden buildings, a walled garden and garden furniture to make from

kits and arrange in ways to suit the seasons are also included. I hope that this book will provide a fund of inspirational ideas as well as the advice and guidance that will help you to carry through your personal project successfully.

Jean Nisbett

Part one
Period houses

Chapter 1
Tudor hunting lodge

For my first project, I have chosen a Tudor-style dolls' house with every detail accurately copied from features seen on real houses dating from the early Tudor period. This is an example of a house that can be purchased ready-built and decorated both outside and in.

Tudor houses have tremendous appeal. The fact that so many have survived for over 400 years is astonishing enough, but when you see a real building, with its oak timbers and gently sagging roof, its plaster infill that may be coloured ochre or terracotta, the ancient glass in the windows, the decorative gable ends and a 16th-century date carved above the lintel, the impression of great age is reinforced.

Now that world travel is so common, visitors to England from overseas are able to marvel at such houses, and the dolls' house hobbyists

among them immediately want to recreate that lost world of the Tudors in 1:12 scale.

This Tudor dolls' house is an ideal choice for the hobbyist who wants to concentrate on furnishing and arranging the rooms to give a lived-in look, or for the collector who may not want to spend time on decoration but instead begin to create a convincing Tudor lifestyle straight away. The project on page 24 is a Tudor dolls' house kit for the hands-on miniaturist who wants to work through the early stages.

1 An authentic Tudor dolls' house in 1:12 scale. It measures 27½in tall to the top of the chimney, 20in wide and approximately 13in deep (700 x 510 x 330mm) including the stone-flagged base. Every detail reproduces the appearance of an early Tudor house.

2 The house as it might be seen from an alleyway in front.

3 An external chimney stack like this one would have been a later addition to such a house, adding to the comfort of its inhabitants

5 The entrance passage is furnished with a bench and a joint stool. On the stairs, an iron rising candlestick holds a candle, placed ready to help ascend the dark, enclosed staircase. (A Tudor rising candlestick could be twisted as the candle burnt down to make the flame more visible.)

King John's Hunting Lodge as inspiration

Years ago I saw an early Tudor house at Axbridge, in Somerset, England, which is known locally as King John's Hunting Lodge. Before planning the furnishings of the dolls' house, I revisited it in search of inspiration, and found that, sadly, local legend is untrue, as this former merchant's house was built around 1500, long after the time of King John of Magna Carta fame. The story had probably grown to explain a carved, crowned wooden head on the corner post, obviously intended to represent a king. But it is now thought that this dates from the 16th or 17th centuries, when for a time the house became the King's Head Tavern.

4 The maker has devised several openings to add interest. A succession of rooms is revealed by removing lift-off panels so that, finally, the whole interior can be seen.

Accurate Tudor style

Everything about this dolls' house is realistic. The timber framing forms the basic structure, with infill in exactly the right shade of greyish-white to suggest the passage of time: the individually made roof tiles are uneven and varied in colour, and the arched entrance door is reminiscent of similar ones on houses from the period that have survived in Somerset and Essex.

Inside, there are two main rooms and an attic under the eaves, an entrance passage and landing with a boxed-in, winding staircase to connect them, and a wall with an arched doorway dividing the passage from the main living room. Although this house is small, it has everything necessary for Tudor life; larger models can also be ordered, finished to the same high standard.

This is too small to be a grand house, but as a hunting lodge it would have belonged to someone of status. I imagined it as a place where the huntsman could stay overnight, with perhaps just one servant and a groom in attendance, to escape from the pressures of a busy household. It is helpful to think of some storyline like this for any dolls' house, as to create an authentic interior you need to imagine the life that might go on inside and arrange the furniture as it would be used.

8 The landing, with its leaded window to let in plenty of light, is large enough for a writing desk and chair. Slipware plates displayed on the wall add interest to a plain interior.

6 An atmospheric view through the archway from the hall to the main room beyond.

Seeing and being able to go inside this ancient building once again gave me a real feeling for how I wanted my own dolls' house to look. I also decided that to use it as the hunting lodge it never was would add even more interest to the project.

7 Chosen to emphasize my planned use of the house as a hunting lodge, a doe hides shyly round a corner. The miniature is made of bronze.

9 The huntsman has returned from a day in the open air, pulled off his boots before the fire and gone upstairs to find his servant and supper. The whippet, originally a hunting dog – here miniaturized in bronze – waits patiently for his master's return.

The parlour

The upstairs parlour is richly furnished with a fine array of pewter and a cupboard with carved and painted Tudor roses on the front panels. The only high-backed chair in the house is next to the writing desk on the landing, but here there are two joint stools, the usual form of seating for most people. I imagine that, under the covered pewter serving dish, the huntsman's supper has been left ready for him to eat.

10 Carpets were far too valuable to be walked on in Tudor England and were more usually draped over tables for display. But placed on the floor of this parlour it adds richness, colour and an appearance of comfort.

The attic bedroom

The groom would sleep in the stable with the horses and the servant in the warmest corner he could find, perhaps near to the dying embers of the fire. The huntsman has, for those times, a more comfortable place.

He would spend the night in the attic room on a low bed known as a 'cant' bed: the style was specifically designed to fit in a room with a sloping ceiling, or it could be tucked under the stairs.

How to complete an unfinished Tudor house

I really enjoyed this project, at least in part because I already had most of the furniture and could quickly see how it would look when in place. Although few makers offer houses that are so fully finished internally, you can achieve similar effects yourself to complete an undecorated doll's house, or one assembled from a kit like the one that features in chapter 2.

Stone flags

Stone floors always look attractive and it is not difficult to make one. The floor will look most realistic if it is slightly uneven.

Method

1 Measure the floor and draw up a template on a piece of card to use as guide.

11 The attic bedroom beneath a roof that has been lifted away. The green-painted coffer would have been old even in Tudor times – but still used to store extra bedding.

12 13 The house with flooring in place. The flagstones were made individually, then painted to suggest wear. You can make your own, using the method described.

14 A planked floor can be enhanced by polishing with a good furniture polish to scent the room with lavender or beeswax, just as it would have been in Tudor times.

2 Make the flagstones from a stone-coloured modelling compound. Roll out the compound into a thin sheet and then score it to make random sizes of flagstones.

3 Harden the compound in the oven, following the pack instructions.

4 Fix the floor in place with wood adhesive or all-purpose glue. Use watered-down acrylic paint to vary the colour, darkening some areas to suggest wear.

5 Finish with a coat of matt varnish to protect the surface.

An easier method is to use tile adhesive which is a greyish-white colour with some variation. Spread it over the floor with a spatula, score with a knife to mark out stone flags in random sizes. Leave to dry.

TIP

If you happen to have some car body filler, this can be used in the same way as tile adhesive.

Wooden floors

Planked floors can be fitted in upper storeys and should be of oak. In real houses from this period, the floors have sometimes acquired an alarming slope that can make you feel queasy as you walk across them, but although the planks should look uneven and show signs of wear, it is best to make the floor level enough to place furniture without having to prop it up at one end.

Although wood flooring sheet is ideal for a dolls' house of a later period, it is too smooth and well-finished for use in a Tudor room. Instead, it is worth taking the trouble to use real oak strip and to cut and lay the planks individually. Thin oak strip is available from model shops, usually in 18in (460mm) lengths, or from hardware stores in 24in (610mm) lengths. A width of about ¾in (19mm) is most suitable as planks used in Tudor times were wider than nowadays. Vary the lengths of the planks – most can be quite long. Use the left-over short pieces randomly so that the effect is not 'bitty'.

Method

---

1 Cut a template from thin card to fit the floor of the room. Colour the card with the same wood stain you intend to use on the planks, or with water-based paint in a similar colour to stop white patches showing through any gaps between planks.

2 Fix the planks to the card with wood adhesive and be careful to remove any excess with a damp cloth immediately as wood stain will not take if used over glue.

3 Leave to dry. Trim any overhangs at the edges and check the fit.

4 For extra realism, make nail marks at the ends of the planks, using an HB pencil, before staining.

15 Vary the lengths of the planks – most can be quite long.

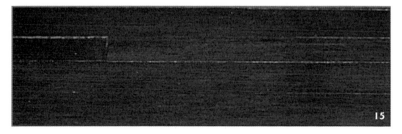

16 This fine example of an inglenook fireplace was provided by the maker of the dolls' house.

5 Make a stone hearth in the same way as a stone floor. Use twigs from the garden to represent logs in the fireplace – to prevent them from crumbling, add a coat of matt varnish before you arrange them.

Ceiling beams

To make beams, use square dowelling from a model shop. You will need two thicknesses, one about ⅜in (10mm) square to provide heavy supporting beams, and one about ¼in (6mm) square for the thinner cross beams in between.

Method

1 Cut the dowel to length and distress it with a hammer before staining. Use either a light or dark oak colour, depending on whether you want a newly built or an aged look for your Tudor house.

An inglenook fireplace

Your house will need a fireplace. A wide inglenook is simple to construct: design it in a size to suit the room. The main feature is the huge bressumer, a heavy oak beam over the front of the fireplace, which helped to support the chimney wall.

Method

1 To make the chimney breast you will need some balsa or other wood about 1–1½in (25–38mm) thick, to run from floor to ceiling. Decide on the height of the aperture for the fire and cut one piece of wood for each side to this height.

2 For the bressumer (cross beam), you will need a thick piece of wood to stain as oak: if you can find an old, battered piece, so much the better. If not then use new strip wood about 1in (25mm) thick and distress it with a small hammer before staining.

3 Cut the top part of the chimney breast from the balsa to the same width and to reach the ceiling from above the cross beam.

4 Line the fireplace opening with plain or herringbone pattern brick sheet. Add a fireback if you wish; these are available in different sizes, made from cast resin or metal.

17 Fitting ceiling beams after cutting, distressing and staining. While working, the house is turned upside down.

18 Panelling and ceiling beams in place. Instead of using paint, an embossed paper is used here as a frieze and on the ceiling to represent plasterwork. If you decide on this option, paint the paper with cream water-based paint to avoid it looking too white against dark panelling.

2 If possible, turn the house on its side or upside down while you glue in the beams – it will be much easier to make sure that they are parallel.

3 Glue the beams in place with all-purpose glue. Do not put in too many – it will look more realistic if they are well spaced out.

Panel a room

Wooden panelling is another option in a Tudor house – perhaps in one room only, as panelling throughout can make the dolls' house look dark. Pre-cut panels, stiles (uprights) and rails (cross pieces) are available from several makers to provide a panelled room without the time-consuming process of cutting out all the pieces yourself. Fitting panelling is fun to do and will look impressive.

Method

1 Measure the room carefully to work out how many panels, stiles and rails you will need. Make a card template to check the fit. Slight adjustments to the size of the panels can be made in the back corners of the room, where a narrower panel will not be noticeable.

2 Decide how far up the wall the panelled section will reach and paint as plaster above this height before fitting. Extend the painted section about ½in (12mm) below the proposed top of the panelling.

3 The stiles and rails can be left plain, but will look much more realistic if they are chamfered (shaped with a flat file) before fitting. This is time-consuming, but easy to do. It does not matter if there are small irregularities in the chamfers, as these will just add to the handmade look.

4 It is important to stain everything with wood stain before fitting, to avoid the possibility of getting glue on to bare wood.

19 Panelling kit as supplied.

20 The finished effect after the stiles and rails have been chamfered with a flat file, then stained.

21

22

21 A fine panelled room might be the best parlour in your Tudor dolls' house.

22 A corner of a panelled room in a manor house. A tapestry hung on the wall provides not only colour but also adds extra warmth.

23 24 A fine example of a late medieval coffer with pierced and carved roundels and a metal catch and keyplate, made by a master miniaturist. Coffers were used for storing clothes, valuables and documents and were often fitted with locks for security and privacy.

23

24

TIP

To give the panelling an old and worn look, lighten the centres of the panels before the stain is dry by rubbing gently with a cloth dampened with white spirit. When fully dry, apply a coat of sanding sealer, allow to dry, then rub down carefully with 0000 steel wool. This will wear away both stain and sealant on the edges of the rails. Finish with two further coats of sanding sealer, then polish.

The furniture

The hunting lodge has all the basic furniture that would have been in use in such a small Tudor house, but if your dolls' house is larger, you will be able to include a few more pieces. You can include furniture from a slightly earlier or later period; late medieval furniture might still have been in use. Jacobean 17th-century furniture could be added to a 16th-century house. Furniture styles changed slowly; pieces were passed on to the next generation, and used until they wore out. It could take years before country craftsmen caught up with the new styles so they simply continued to make the designs they knew best.

26 Another useful piece is a settle with storage space under the seat. The panelled back would not make for comfort, but did keep out draughts.

27 Who could resist this appealing hanging cradle, made with such care to include turned finials on the end posts and linenfold panels?

25 One essential piece of furniture was an aumbry, a tall cupboard with a carved front, pierced to provide ventilation. It would originally have been used for storing food, but gradually aumbries were also used for storing linen, as here, or in wealthy households, for books.

28 A panelled chest for general use. The mugs and platters laid out on top are of pewter. Although the chest is plain, pewter was reserved for gentry, as ordinary folk would have drunk from leather or wooden mugs.

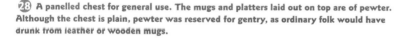

29 The handsome stool in the parlour is an elaborately carved piece with pierced roundels and carved legs, reinforcing the impression that the huntsman is wealthy.

30 Elaborate pewter makes a fine impression on this long table and bench. The gleam of pewter, especially when seen by candlelight, added a decorative element to Tudor rooms.

Painted furniture

Late medieval painted furniture might still be in use in an early Tudor house. Red and green were favoured colours and ornamentation in off-white or even gold was highly decorative.

If you want to include some painted furniture, try painting a plain whitewood chest in dark red or green with matt acrylic paint.

31 A late medieval coffer, in use in the attic of the hunting lodge, was made and painted by the maker of the dolls' house and is based on an original design.

32

33

32 As you can tell from the small number of pieces, this is a really easy kit to make up.

33 A bench has many uses – in an entrance passage, in the parlour or on a landing.

Ceiling beams were sometimes painted in a simple running design, again usually in red or green. This is easy to do but with the low ceilings of most dolls' houses you might find that it will not be very visible – check out first whether you can see the undersides of any beams without stooping down.

34 This kit has more pieces to glue together, but the instructions are easy to follow.

35 Take your time and you will have a fine chair for the master of the house.

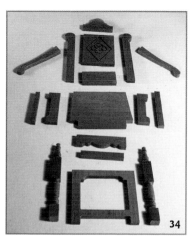

34

Furniture to assemble from kits

Another way to provide suitable furniture is to make some of it from kits. Here are two nice examples: neither is difficult to assemble, but bear in mind that the finishing of a furniture kit is all-important if it is

35

to look as good as pieces made by a professional miniaturist. (For more on furniture kits, see page 167.)

The Tudor age continues to fascinate us; every few years a new film or TV series will be made about Henry VIII or Elizabeth I. Most films are about life in the royal palaces but miniaturizing a more ordinary Tudor home will be a satisfying project for a hobbyist.

Bear in mind that you do not need many pieces of furniture, as even large rooms were sparsely furnished. Add colour and warmth with tapestry hangings and pewter, bowls of flowers or pot pourri; polish wooden floors with lavender-scented polish or beeswax, and enjoy your Tudor-style dolls' house.

Chapter 2
Stratford Place bakery

This original dolls' house and market space is assembled from a kit. It is more sophisticated than the early Tudor model in chapter 1, but it is equally authentic, based on houses dating from the second part of the 16th century. The kit illustrates a wide range of techniques that may be required in kit assembly.

When I was young I lived near to Stratford-upon-Avon, England, and still make frequent visits, so I was delighted to find a dolls' house with such attention to detail in such a familiar style.

The house has an attractive exterior staircase with a 'catslide' roof (a sloping roof covering an extension), both common features of buildings from the Tudor period, plus a very usable covered outside space. These features are not exclusive to this particular dolls' house, and will

① Stratford Place Bakery is a splendid example of a dolls' house based on a 16th-century building.

also be found on other Tudor-style dolls' houses, although there are some differences.

Two things to note are that the roof construction is complicated, so might be difficult for a beginner to tackle without some help; and there are approximately 130 beams and mouldings to stain and glue in place, which requires some patience.

The kit assembly

As with any kit, start by identifying the main sections, then go through the instructions and diagrams twice

② The covered outside staircase was commonly used to reach the upper storey and allowed for furniture to be taken up. Inside the house, a ladder and a trapdoor was often the only way to reach a bedroom or storeroom.

3 An outdoor covered area is useful for market stalls or animals.

4 Always check and identify the parts of a kit before you begin to assemble it and make sure that you read the instructions carefully.

to make sure that you understand exactly what to do. Next, do a 'dry build' – fitting the parts together to see how they join when you repeat this process using glue.

TIP

The recommended 'dry build' time of two hours refers to the main structure, and is not intended as a guide to how long it will take to complete the whole house, with all the additions.

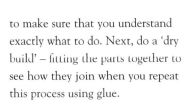

5 Masking tape in different widths will keep parts together while the glue sets. A wooden triangle is useful to check that corners are square and that the assembly does not lean.

The main carcass assembly is straightforward. You will find that the adhesive provided (wood-glue) dries quickly, so wipe off any excess immediately with a damp cloth, then hold the joins together with masking tape until fully dry. Before putting the pillars in place at a later stage, the upper room extension

literally hangs in space and seems to defy gravity. But you can be certain that the makers will have tested out an assembly thoroughly before marketing a dolls' house kit, so there is no need for alarm. I did, however, take the precaution of propping up the overhang with the pillars while the adhesive dried.

6 Part of the dry build, held together by adhesive putty and masking tape.

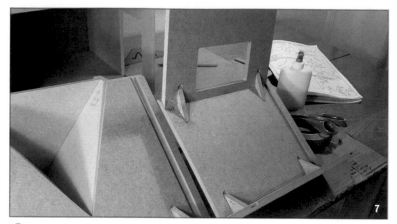

(8) The roof assembly propped up while the glue sets.

(7) In this kit, the roof construction is unusual, with the front wall of the room over the market area attached so that it opens up when the roof is lifted up. Triangular wedges have been used to attach the two sections.

The roof assembly

On first reading through, I found the instructions for the roof assembly unclear. If you are confused when starting any assembly procedure, a second reading (and perhaps a cup of coffee) will usually clarify matters. As a woodworker friend once said to me: 'The person who writes the instructions knows what they mean, because they have already done it, but they are not always quite so obvious to the person reading them.' This part of the assembly is simple.

(9) The overhanging section is firmly secured in place.

Wooden triangles fit into slots and, once glued, wedge the sections together firmly. This would probably be easier with two pairs of hands, so a fellow hobbyist (or anyone else who can be persuaded to help) would be useful at this point. In any case, working with a friend on a kit assembly is fun and discussion and laughter are preferable to frustration while you work out what to do.

Identifying the timbers

The large number of timbers and small wooden pieces are bagged up separately for each section, with a list of contents in each bag. Even so, some of the smaller pieces are remarkably similar, with minuscule differences in length or shape, and it is not immediately clear which is which, or where they fit, by referring to the printed information.

A useful method, when tackling any kit that has many small wooden additions, is to fix each piece temporarily in place with adhesive putty, to check that they are all

correctly in position. Once you are certain, number each piece on the reverse in pencil.

Timbers must be stained before gluing in place. Wood stain is water-based and can be applied with a brush or with a small piece of clean white cloth. A brush can be washed with water and detergent; you may choose to wear plastic gloves during the application. The advantage of building a half-timbered kit house is that you can paint the exterior walls before adding the timbers.

(10) To fit the beams on the underside of the room over the market space, I found it easier to lay the house on its back so that I could see clearly how to space them.

⑪ The construction looks as though it has been made by a master carpenter!

Fitting the staircase

Stain the stairs before fixing in place: for this type of covered Tudor staircase they were usually of wood, not stone. Water-based stain has a tendency to make wood swell slightly, so you may find it necessary to sand the edges down a little in order to fit the stairs neatly between the house wall and the staircase wall. Hinge on the façade following the instructions; two pairs of hands may be helpful.

⑫ The stairs are in place and the 'catslide' roof is yet to be added. Timbers are tried out for position, held temporarily in place with adhesive putty.

⑬ The timbers are now correctly positioned and glued in place.

⑭ The overhanging jetty and lattice-paned windows are impressive. Here the façade is laid flat so these features can be added.

Decorating the exterior

These suggestions for exterior decoration will apply to any Tudor or Elizabethan house. Probably the most familiar treatment to many readers will be the white (or off-white) plastered walls and blackened timbers that are pictured in so many tourist guide books – but note that the darkened timbers were a Victorian fashion that is now out of favour with conservationists.

For a more authentic appearance, most of the Tudor and Elizabethan houses in Shakespeare's Stratford-upon-Avon have been carefully restored to resemble their original appearance, with timbering returned to natural oak that has darkened with age to a greyish tone. But not everyone follows this procedure: towards the Welsh borders, in Herefordshire, black and white remains supreme. So the choice is yours, and whichever you prefer will look splendid on your dolls' house.

For my own house, I chose a walnut wood stain to simulate a medium oak – it is warm without being too dark. It is always preferable to choose wood stain by its true colour – not by what it says on the can. Test it on a spare piece of wood to judge the effect.

The exterior walls are painted an off-white colour – a mixture of white and peach-toned water-based paint. Alternative colours that are often used on the walls are ochre or Suffolk pink, which is a terracotta that can vary from pale to almost red. This has traditionally been used as limewash on houses not only in Suffolk, but also in many other parts of England.

Brick cladding

Another authentic treatment for the exterior walls of a Tudor house is to add brick cladding, either on the lower part of the façade or

15 Brick cladding sheet is a simple way to add texture and colour to parts of a house front. A traditional herringbone pattern is useful for infill between upright timbers, or to provide a fireplace back.

16 An example of roof tiles that have variations in the colour.

17 The interior has been decorated and is now ready to try out furnishing ideas.

between timbers – provided these are vertical, as on this house. In theory, brick cladding can be added in the space between curved timbers, but it is harder to achieve a neat fit.

Brick cladding can be cut with scissors or a craft knife. Make a paper pattern, check the fit carefully and adjust it if necessary before cutting the cladding.

The roof

The roof can be painted or clad with textured tiling in sheet form. Choose grey slate, or russet to represent clay tiles. Ready-made slates and tiles are supplied in packs and can be fixed in place individually, which is time-consuming but not difficult. If you plan to do this, note that shingles (shaped tiles) are unsuitable on a Tudor roof. Plain, fibre tiles are lightweight and easy to fix.

To fix individual roof tiles, use PVA adhesive. Start at the bottom edge of the roof, overlapping each row by about ¼in (6mm), staggering the tiles so that there is a half tile at the end of alternate rows.

Interior decoration

This kit is named Stratford Place bakery – an inventive idea for a possible use. It can also be arranged as a dwelling house or a shop, with either living accommodation or storage on the upper floor. It is not a grand building, so the interior walls would have been colour-washed, like any cottage of the time. Off-white, ochre or terracotta, as used on the outside, are all suitable shades.

Flooring

In a cottage-style building such as this one, the downstairs floor might originally have been of beaten earth – which can be simulated with textured paint – or it would have been made of brick. Alternatively, you might prefer to create a flagstone floor, using one of the methods given in the previous section. In the upstairs rooms, wooden planked floors are obligatory. I have used a rich, dark stain on the floorboards in this house.

18 A brick floor can be laid in one piece. Planks upstairs are stained dark. The modern sink is an idea for a possible update for 21st-century living.

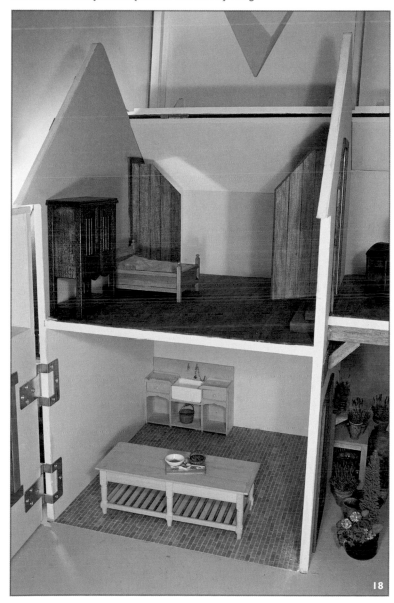

19

20

21

Fittings

The bakery would be in an outhouse or lean-to extension because of the fire risk, but in a cottage home you might like to add a fireplace with a stone hearth.

Furniture

For a bakery you can include plain wooden tables and simple kitchen equipment and, of course, some newly baked bread.

A bedroom used solely for sleeping would have been unimaginable in a small Tudor home, when often an entire family including children slept in one bed, nose to tail. But the dolls' house has two upper rooms, and this gives the hobbyist an opportunity to provide a master bedroom and a second bedroom.

If the upwardly mobile household has a parlour, you can include some nicely polished furniture too. Here are some pieces that would suit such a room.

19 A stone fireplace for the better-off householder. The brick is nicely smoke-blackened to show use: paint and smudge on a black/grey acrylic paint mix to achieve this effect.

20 This homely kitchen would suit either a bakery or a cottage home.

21 An idea for an upstairs room, combining sleeping accommodation with a storeroom. A rough blanket and pillow on the bed suggest a little added comfort.

23

24

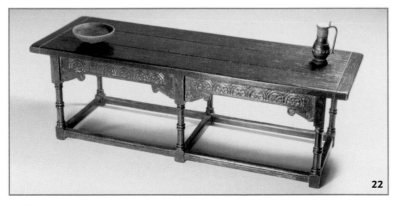

22

22 A long table with a planked top has turned legs and a carved frieze.

23 A wall-hung storage cupboard kept food out of the reach of vermin. The turned uprights on this nicely distressed version show that it would have belonged to a reasonably well-off household.

24 Decorated slipware pots make a change from the ubiquitous pewter and add a touch of colour to the table.

An outside space

Merchants' houses often had a covered space for market stalls in the pillared area below the jettied upper floor, and my bakery includes a similar space that can be put to a range of uses by the miniaturist. Try laying out freshly baked bread from the bakery on simple trestle tables and piling fresh vegetables up in baskets or onto a cart.

It might also be a useful place to tether a horse or keep a guard dog, or chickens in a pen. A weekly stock market has been a feature of small

towns since the 12th century, and you might prefer to have a shepherd with some sheep for sale. Take your pick!

Make a market cart from a kit

A market cart piled high with vegetables is still a common sight in market towns today, as it was in the 16th century. Here is a nice example to make up from a simple whitewood kit.

25 Fancy breads from the bakery are sure to attract customers, displayed in a shallow basket with a neatly plaited edge.

26 English cheeses mature on a plain wooden table.

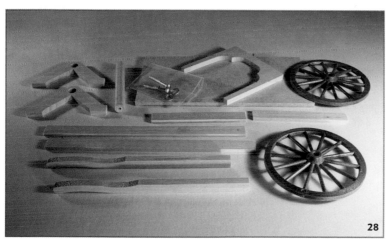

27 An example of another covered area, attached to a larger Tudor house, where there is enough space for livestock and a log pile.

28 The market cart kit is simplicity itself to assemble.

29 Piled high with vegetables, the market cart will make a colourful centrepiece for the market space.

Chapter 3
Heal's shop conversion

In this example of a conversion project, I turn a small 19th-century shop premises into a 21st-century home. It was bought, over 20 years ago, from Heal's long-established furniture store in London, where each year in the run-up to Christmas, a toy department was opened for a short time.

Although designed for a child to play with, the façade is noteworthy, as it was based on Heal's own first store in Tottenham Court Road, which had opened there in 1818 after moving from smaller premises nearby. Heal's must have been quite proud of their dolls' house, as it is mentioned in a history of the company, published in 1984.

The exterior decoration

The dolls' house is made of plywood. In order to provide a smooth surface without obscuring the distinctive black lettering, I used satin-finish varnish. This is also a good choice if you want to give a dolls' house an antique appearance. I applied seven coats of varnish to achieve an

impermeable sheen and, after more than 20 years, when I decided to alter the interior decorations, the exterior still looked as good as new. The only upkeep it required was an occasional rub with a soft duster.

To varnish the exterior of a dolls' house, you need to aim for a surface that looks and feels like satin, so you will need several coats until you are satisfied with the finish. To varnish successfully, you need a slightly different technique from painting.

Method

1 Imagine that you are floating the varnish over the surface of the wood, rather than brushing it in. I use a ¾in (19mm) paintbrush.

2 Varnish is easier to apply if it is not too cold. If it has been kept in a cold place, do not use the varnish until you have brought it to average room temperature by keeping it indoors for a few hours before use.

3 Varnish gives off fumes so it is important to work in a well-ventilated room. A dust-free atmosphere is important while varnish dries because it seems to attract any small particles, and these will spoil the finish.

1 The attractive and unusual façade of the Heal's dolls' house and shop reproduces the original 19th-century lettering, copied from an early print.

2 The dolls' house was designed to withstand children's play. As supplied, the solid front door opened outwards and the panels were merely drawn on in black. I wanted to change this so I used coloured varnish to make a feature of it.

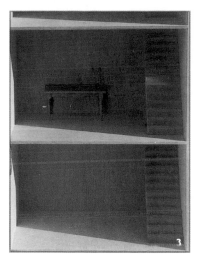

3 The smooth plywood finish of the interior before decoration. It is provided with a basic staircase without balusters, newel post or handrail.

4 Do not use a brush that you have previously used to apply paint – any flecks will be drawn out by the varnish. Start with a fresh brush.

5 Brush on with light, smooth strokes. Always work in the same direction, with the grain of the wood, and never go back over an area that you have just varnished. Wait until the next coat to cover up any patches that have been missed.

6 Rub down lightly between coats with the finest grade of sandpaper or finishing paper. Finally, for a really smooth finish, rub over gently with a soft cloth before polishing with a good quality furniture polish.

The conversion

The dolls' house is based on a modest town house, which would have been one of a terrace of similar small houses. In early 19th-century London such a house might have been arranged with a shop or workshop on the entrance floor, while the owner lived above, just like the original Heal's. So my first interior scheme, in Georgian style, was arranged in this way.

Today, most artisans' houses such as this have been converted into modern homes, so the interiors are markedly different from what you might expect. When I decided to celebrate the millennium by updating my dolls' house I thought that it would be interesting to have a change of use as well as style, and make a conversion from 19th-century shop into a 21st-century home.

This project illustrates some of the problems you might come across in any conversion of this kind, and explains how to solve them.

4 Before conversion: the shop floor as I first arranged it. It appeared that the bedding store also sold dolls' houses.

5 The new front door: a wood sample in fumed oak made a plain door and the surround is of stripwood, painted matt black to coordinate with the lettering on the façade. I fitted a shop-bought modern handle. A 'spy hole' and an entry phone were adapted from metal oddments from my bits box.

6 The inside of the new plain front door is painted to match the updated staircase. The inside front is varnished to match the exterior.

The only change I made to the façade was to provide a new front door, as the original had been designed to be childproof rather than accurate. Under current building regulations for historic properties, my alteration to such a prominent feature would not be allowed, but there are no restrictions on such changes to a dolls' house!

The staircase

The staircase had always been a slight problem, because each flight stopped short of the floor above. Fortunately they are at the side, so this is not really noticeable. I planned a modern open staircase to give a more spacious feeling to the small rooms, which meant removing all the balusters and the handrail.

This was simple: as I had put them in place initially I knew that they were glued on to the basic staircase and not pegged in so that it would be easy to snap them off, then sand the steps smooth. But in general, in such a conversion, it is better to keep the original staircase and repaint or stain it to suit your new scheme, rather than risk damage.

Method

1 Remove any traces of glue left from fixed-down carpet with white spirit and wire wool. Wear rubber gloves to protect your hands.

2 Sand thoroughly, then wipe over with white spirit to provide a clean, smooth surface for repainting.

3 Repaint with satin-finish paint or, for a metallic finish, apply two coats of metallic model enamel, allowing six hours' drying time between coats.

4 Finally, buff up the finish using a soft cloth.

Planning the new decorations

Once the stairs were modernized, I enjoyed planning the new decorations. These were inspired by seeing schemes for similar updates featured in interiors magazines and

7 Clean, light colours and metallic finishes make the interior look fresh and modern. In the corners of the rooms, paper cut-outs are used to check out the space available for kitchen units.

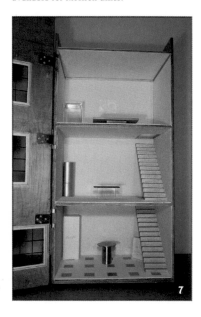

also by my son's recent conversion of his London apartment. Here are a few points to bear in mind if you plan a modern scheme.

• A small house, when opened to view, will always look more spacious if room colours are coordinated.

• To get a good finish when using water-based paint in pastel colours, it is important to apply a white undercoat first, in order to provide a clean foundation. This is also a good idea before pasting up the wallpaper.

• Flooring can be simulated with regular scale vinyl wallpaper. Although not so hardwearing as wood, it will make an adequate floor for a hobbyist who will treat it gently. There are some attractive patterns that mimic tiles or textured carpet (examples are in my house) and a sample may be large enough to complete a room.

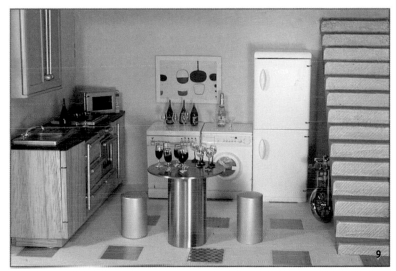

8 The house is presented as though the new owner has just moved in, so there are no personal possessions scattered around. Contrary to appearances, the textured carpet in the sitting room is wallpaper. The paintings on the walls came from greeting cards.

9 Filled wine glasses and bottles are laid out in the kitchen, ready for the house-warming party.

10 All the kitchen units can be opened to reveal well-fitted interiors. One unit incorporates sink, cooker and cupboards, which suits the limited space better than individual units. There is even room for a microwave on the work surface.

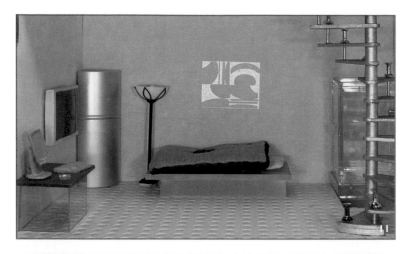

11 The bedroom is calm and restful. A pearlized wallpaper with a single large motif on the wall above the bed adds vitality to the largely monochrome scheme. The floor-standing lamp is from a range of dolls' house lighting that includes modern as well as period designs.

12 The finished interior looks just as I had hoped it would. I added a spiral staircase on the bedroom floor, to reach a new roof garden, and tucked a shower cubicle behind the stairs.

13 This iconic lounger is instantly recognizable as the work of Le Corbusier, and suits a modern room.

14 The Wassily chair was designed by Marcel Breuer; a trend-setting piece in its time, it is much admired by furniture designers and reproductions are still made today.

Modern furniture

Many contemporary designs of dolls' house furniture are well made and will look upmarket in a 21st-century room. You should have no difficulty in finding just what you want in dolls' house shops or through mail order outlets. There is now greater interest in designs that were

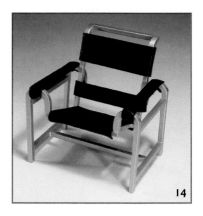

15

16

17

15 A 'director's chair' will find a place in most modern interiors. Like a real chair, this miniature version can be folded.

16 A rush-seated chair designed by Vico Magistretti, which was marketed by Terence Conran in his Habitat stores in the 1960s. It has become a design classic and would fit well into a 21st-century home. We still have a full-size set and I can vouch for them being comfortable.

17 A well-designed, wall-hung unit containing both shelves and cupboards. This is based on a full-size modern unit. Two coats of acrylic paint create a pleasing finish.

18 The stylish bed can be assembled in minutes.

19 You can buy a 1:12 shower unit, but this version is intended to look as minimalist as possible, to suit the ultra-modern scheme.

considered avant garde when they first appeared in the early 20th century and miniatures makers have followed suit by reproducing them in 1:12 scale.

Economy ideas for furniture

For the kitchen, you might like to paint some plain modern cupboards in a colour to suit your scheme.

Easy, money-saving ideas often work well when providing modern furniture. Many everyday items can be adapted – the following examples are all in my house.

- The kitchen table is a metal container that was originally used to hold cocktail sticks, turned upside down; the stools are bottle caps.

- The bed is an acrylic box topped with a piece of smooth, polished wood plus a pillow and 'duvet'. The duvet is a velvet and linen lavender bag.

- The shower cubicle is also made out of an acrylic pencil box. Plastic washers provide a plug-hole and door handle, while the token shower head is a circular metal nut taken from my bits box.

- The sofa in the sitting room is made from three fabric-covered, padded boxes, which are widely available from gift shops in a variety of patterns (see page 38).

18

19

🔟 The sofa is quick and easy to make.

Make a sofa

You will need three fabric-covered boxes with padded tops. Mine measured 2¾ x 2¾ x ¾in high (70 x 70 x 19mm).

Method

1 Draw a line across the centre of one box, complete with lid, and cut it in half using a craft knife and raised-edge metal ruler. To prevent the fabric cover from fraying, run a thin line of all-purpose glue along the cut edges.

2 Glue the sides of the box halves together to form the seat base. To make the sofa back, glue the remaining two boxes together side by side. Then glue the cut-open edges of the base to the sofa back.

3 Add glass or metal stick pins (from a stationer's) at each corner of the base to make the feet.

Make a spiral staircase from a kit

The advantage of a house with a flat roof is that you can add a roof garden. To reach it, I installed a spiral staircase assembled from a kit and placed it at the side of the bedroom over the main staircase.

The kit I used was originally designed to make a traditional spiral staircase for a basement area or inside a shop. Wooden treads, a brass chain, brass spacers or thin rod, handrail and turned brass finials are all provided with this kit. The instructions are clear and easy to follow, and a picture of the finished staircase is included.

The central brass rod can be shortened if you need less height. I found this easy to do, using a saw and mitre box (see page 156). Note that it is best to use a different saw blade for metal than the one you use to saw wooden mouldings, as metal will blunt it very quickly. Saw blades are inexpensive and they are easy to fit into the handle.

You can adapt this staircase, or one from a similar kit, for placing in a modern room.

Method

1 Sand the treads thoroughly, then paint them with two coats of matt metallic model enamel, allowing six hours' drying time between coats. Then buff up with a soft cloth.

2 Shorten each stair spacer rod so that the top is level with the top of the tread above. You will not need to use the chain and finials provided, which are sure to come in useful for another purpose – I used mine to complete some railings.

3 Paint the brass rods with two coats of matt metallic model enamel to match the treads, or leave them as brass if preferred.

🔟 The kit parts to assemble the spiral staircase. The treads have been painted, ready for the spacers to be added.

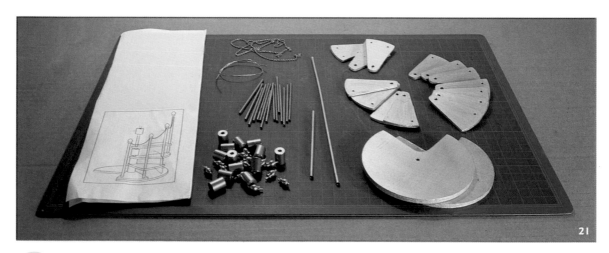

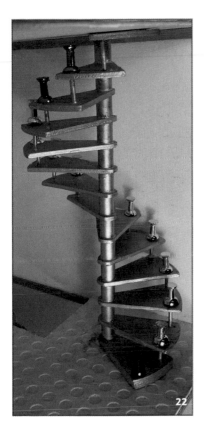

22 The completed spiral staircase will look as though it provides access to the roof garden.

In real life it would be contrary to safety regulations to install a spiral staircase without a handrail, but it does add a light, airy quality to a minimalist interior.

The roof garden

To suit the modern scheme inside the house, the garden has a distinctly Zen look. A roof garden can be added to any dolls' house with a suitable flat roof.

1 To make decking, fit strips of balsa or any stripwood and paint them with a coat of matt varnish to keep the natural look.

2 To make a windbreak, use webbing from a haberdasher's.

3 To simulate trapdoor access, top a shallow acrylic box with a piece of plain wood and position it over the top of the staircase that is inside the house.

4 Provide a hot tub as a centrepiece. These are available ready-made, but for economy, make one from a round box painted with a metallic finish model enamel, and fill it with simulated water.

5 To complete the tranquil effect, add some pebbles and a few clipped bushes or trees.

The new, modern scheme for the whole house makes a refreshing change from the former period-style decorations. Some of my treasured Georgian furniture, used in this house before the conversion, now features in the larger Georgian-style house in chapter 4.

4 To fit the spiral neatly into a corner, as in this house, fit a double tread at the base rather than the circular base provided, which will take up too much space. The central brass rod will need to be shortened to fit inside a room, and there will be some treads left over.

5 To complete the effect, fix a metallic stick pin to each step. The spacers are hollow, so the pins can be glued inside and through to the tread to fix them firmly in place.

TIP

While working on the kit, it can be fixed down securely with a piece of adhesive putty to keep it steady.

---

23 The garden would be an oasis of tranquillity on the roof of a town house, shielded from traffic noise far below by the parapet.

Chapter 4
Classical Georgian house

During the 18th and early 19th centuries, sons of the English nobility were sent on a Grand Tour of Europe to learn about art, sculpture and architecture. These tours resulted not only in wealthy young men shipping home works of art that would later decorate their mansions, but also instilled in them a love of Greek sculpture and the Renaissance architecture of Italy, which inspired the Neoclassical style.

Britain's architectural heritage benefited, with magnificent stately homes in the countryside, and in our towns and cities, Georgian buildings that were also based on similar proportions to those of the outstanding Palladian architecture of 16th-century Italy. In addition to the building of new houses, many existing timber-framed buildings were re-fronted in this new Georgian style. Most of these are easy to pick out, as little effort was made to conceal the overhanging jettied upper storeys, or to alter the Tudor brickwork at the back.

The classical style

A dolls' house in this style always looks good: the Palladian façade scales down to 1:12 size without any changes, to provide a perfect small replica. It is no wonder that this is still the most popular choice for many hobbyists, and that professional miniaturists delight in making Georgian furniture to fill the well-proportioned rooms.

Portland Square

Portland Square is a grand name for the grandest house in my own collection. Based on a typical house in Bath, England (also known as the 'Georgian City'), it measures 48in high x 30in wide x 16½in deep (1220 x 760 x 420mm), extended by 10in (255mm) at the front by a portico and double entrance staircase. There are six large rooms, a central staircase with hall and landings, and a two-room basement – an optional addition.

I built it from a kit – not without difficulty, because the size of the dolls' house made it hard for me to

1 The impressive exterior of the Georgian dolls' house, plainly painted in a stone colour, with details in a paler stone.

2 The porch, completed with columns and a pediment, is characteristic of Georgian architecture. Over the door, a decorative fanlight allows light into the hall. A huge variety of fanlight designs were produced, and served to visually identify each house in a street of terraced houses, before the addition of numbers when the postal service was introduced.

3 The shell of the house is assembled first, and provides useful storage for small parts and equipment while additional assemblies are carried out.

4 The floors are laid and work on internal fittings continues with the addition of door cases, before cutting skirting boards to fit against them.

5 The porch assembly consists of a large number of parts. The completed porch is shown opposite.

turn it round or tip it on to its back during assembly – but other than that, there were no problems.

This particular example is no longer available but the same method of assembly is followed in many other plywood kits. Similar Georgian-style dolls' houses are produced as kits (and ready-built) by other makers, so that it will be easy to find one in a size to suit your requirements.

You will find information and guidance on how to assemble a plywood kit, as well as a separate basement, which is a useful addition provided by several dolls' house makers, on pages 159–162. But in this project, I want to concentrate on the decoration and furnishing of a gentleman's residence in the early 19th century. Suggestions are given and carried through for appropriate flooring and suitable wallpaper patterns (and where to source them). There are also lots of ideas for completing the rooms that would be in daily use and those used for entertaining.

6 The imposing double entrance steps are completed with 'stone' balusters and handrail. The steps rest against the basement front and fit neatly under the porch above, so that they can be lifted off easily when the basement is opened.

7 How the interior might appear as a well-furnished family home.

A grand tour of No. 1 Portland Square

The rooms are decorated as though newly completed in 1815, with wallpapers and paint colours based on similar, still-existing historic

Designing the interior

Following my usual practice, I arranged a sequence of rooms that flow from one to another in the way in which they would have been used. The decorations and furnishing are arranged to suit the lifestyle of my imagined family, living nearly 200 years ago, soon after Jane Austen's novel *Pride and Prejudice* was published.

The comfortable sofas and large library table and the paintings that hang on the walls would have been the personal choices of husband and wife. The small accessories in everyday use, the children's toys and the kitchen equipment and handyman's tools, have all been selected to evoke a way of living that we can only read about in books, or see brought to life in costume dramas.

When I look into this house, every detail now complete, it evokes for me the presence of these imagined inhabitants, as I hope it will for you.

houses. As I live in Bath, a World Heritage Georgian city, I had plenty of opportunity for research without going far from my home, which was also built in 1815.

Inside, the entrance hall is papered with a creamy marbled paper. Real marble was often simulated in scagliola, either to save expense, or in some cases because marble was considered too heavy for its planned use. Scagliola was a pigmented mixture of plaster and marble chippings, cast into panels or columns and then polished. It is so realistic that the only way to detect that it is a composition and not genuine marble is to tap it. In a dolls' house, textured paper with a marbled pattern looks equally realistic, while marble floors can be simulated with sheets of plasticized flooring.

To the right of the hall, there is a neat and clean kitchen. The Georgian kitchen did not have much equipment, and this one is deliberately arranged to look very tidy. There are two kinds of hobbyist: those who prefer the distressed, well-used look; and those who like their dolls' houses to look as though newly decorated, ready for the family to move in. The latter is my own approach: I like the way everything stays pristine without any need for cleaning, unlike my own home.

Kitchen walls were whitewashed or painted off-white. In this dolls' house kitchen I used a wallpaper with a faint self-pattern, so that the walls do not look too smooth. The paintwork is grey-green and the natural, unstained wooden floor has a well-scrubbed look.

On the other side of the hall, there is a study that is also used as a breakfast room. The wallpaper is copied from an archive pattern, and is also a personal favourite. There is a leather chair for the master of the house and a wide armchair covered in striped silk for his wife, allowing space for her long dress to drape without becoming creased.

8 A handsome gilded lantern was the usual hall light at the time, and a marble-topped side table with an important painting hanging over it was the standard choice for hall furniture. The table was a useful place to leave calling cards, generally on a silver salver.

9 The high-ceilinged kitchen looks light and airy and there is food in preparation on the tables. You can easily imagine the bustle of activity when cooking begins.

10 The sets of bookshelves, joined together to fit the width of the study, are from an inexpensive range of furniture. They provide a display area for wood turned goblets, oriental-style porcelain jars and bronze sculptures as well as books.

⓫ On the first floor landing, there is space for a bust on a marbled pedestal and a chair for a waiting attendant.

⓬ Well-polished furniture, landscape paintings and shelves of Georgian glass make an attractive setting for a meal. The painted wooden lemon tree dummy board hides a grate that is empty in summer months.

On the next floor up, on the right of the landing is the dining room, sited over the kitchen so that we can assume a jib door and back staircase to carry up food and clear it away. The meal seems to have reached the after-dinner port stage and fruit is available from a side table. This is an economical way to arrange a dining room for family use, because you do not need a large table, as you would if guests were present. It also allows more space for other furniture.

On the opposite side of the landing, the drawing room also functions as a music room for after-dinner entertainment with a harp and a square piano. A portrait of the daughter of the house hints at the presence of a family that is only just out of sight. The portrait was reduce-photocopied from a reproduction of a painting by Angelica Kauffman of Miss Henrietta Laura Pulteney, who was a notable of Georgian Bath. (She was later created Countess of Bath in her own right.)

13 The drawing room is decorated in pale yellow, picked out with gold, a favoured colour scheme for rooms where company might be present. The mirror over the fireplace is a miniature reproduction of one that still hangs in No. 1 Royal Crescent, Bath, a house that has been preserved with much of its original furniture.

14 The portrait on this landing is of Sir William Holburne, who also had connections with Bath. He was obviously as handsome as he was wealthy. How I wish I could have met him!

The upper landing has a more homely feeling, with a useful chest of drawers for storage. The picture above could be of the school attended by an older son of the family. Over the stairs, a painting of his father looks benignly down.

On the left of the landing is the elegantly decorated bedroom with its obligatory four-poster bed, a pole screen by the fireplace and gentleman's wig on its stand.

Opposite to the main bedroom, the pretty nursery is shared by a younger daughter and her baby brother. Toys are scattered around as though in play, and there is a very special 1:144th scale dolls' house that can, in turn, be opened to show the rooms inside. I plan to make some furniture, inevitably somewhat simplified in construction, to display in this house.

15 On the chaise longue at the foot of the bed, a novel by Jane Austen might be read while taking a cup of tea, the fashionable drink of the time.

16 Paintings, especially portraits, appeared in most rooms of a Georgian house, before photography gave us instant likenesses of family and friends.

The picture in a gilded frame is of the Gower family children, painted by George Romney in 1766, again reduce-photocopied and framed in replica picture-frame moulding. We may assume that these children are relatives of the family, and that by the date of this house they would be grown up.

17 A beautifully finished dolls' house complete with metal railings and balcony, in the style of a Parisian mansion.

18 In the servants' hall, the painted settle is close to the fire, while the Orkney chair is reserved for the butler, who I imagine to be Scottish. Both forms of seating were designed to exclude drafts.

19 A child's sleigh and a small carriage are stored near to the double back doors so that they can be taken out easily.

The servants' quarters

The two-room basement is arranged with a servants' hall in the larger room and an adjoining space used by the outdoor servants. The servants' hall provides a place for them to relax all-too-briefly, after the day's work. They must have a kindly employer, as the room is more comfortably furnished than most at the time, and it has the luxury of a fire.

The room used by the gardener and handyman has to serve several purposes. It is also a coach house,

a repository for outdoor games for the family, and a place to use the garden's large crop of apples by making cider. Flowering plants are sheltered in here when the weather is cold, and boots next to the kitchen door will no doubt be cleaned by the handyman.

Fitting out a Georgian house

Using this featured dolls' house as an example, here is some guidance on how to complete the interior as it might have looked in the early 19th century. The details reflect the living arrangements in a large house, where the servants' domain was the basement (or sometimes, the attics) and the principal rooms for entertainment were on the 'piano nobile' or first upper floor.

Today, many houses originally lived in by a single family, and now too large for life without servants, have been divided into apartments, but the period details such as architraves, fireplaces, six-panel doors and elaborate door cases remain unchanged, or restored, to enhance the surroundings of modern residents. All these details can be reproduced in a dolls' house and will give lasting pleasure.

Flooring

Marble tiles in the entrance hall were generally laid in the classic design of white or cream squares divided with small black diamonds. 'Marble' flooring is available in plasticized sheet that can be cut with scissors to fit the space, and in a dolls' house it looks almost as

good as the real thing. Cream and black tiles create a warmer effect than white and black, and in the dolls' house give a better impression of period style.

Deal (pine) floors were laid in servants' rooms, but oak can be used in all the principal rooms. Kitchen floors were scrubbed over with sand to remove grease, then swept carefully. I used the same wood flooring sheet as used in the other rooms, but left it unstained and unpolished.

The general rule was that beyond the best rooms where company might be entertained, less expensive materials were used: children's rooms, like servants' rooms and attic rooms, might also have 'deal' floors for economy. In a dolls' house where you can see all the rooms at once I prefer to use the same flooring throughout if possible, so the nursery too has an oak floor.

20 Tiled flooring is laid in the entrance hall and work is in progress, cutting and fitting architraves to provide door frames.

21 The light floorboards are intended to give the effect of a newly sanded and scrubbed floor. The centrepiece of this kitchen is the glorious range, with its burnished metal trim and high shelf above. I chose it in preference to a black-leaded range set into a large fireplace, which would have given it a Victorian appearance.

Basement rooms

Basements were always flagstoned, but sometimes boards were laid on top at a later date. When I moved into my London home of roughly the same period, I was astonished to find flagstones under the linoleum that had been fitted in the basement kitchen by the previous owners. Needless to say, this particular kitchen swiftly became a boiler room! In my servants' hall, the planked floor gives a little more comfort to weary feet.

For the outdoor servants' room, I laid real miniature ceramic flagstones. These are easy to glue in place with PVA adhesive, but are unlikely to fit a room exactly. They should not be laid in regular squares; they are supplied in packs of square or rectangular flagstones, and using some of each will give a pleasing effect. Work out how you want to place them, then use a fine saw blade to cut off any excess at the edges of the room. Do this carefully, as they are likely to crumble if treated roughly. If one does crack across you might use it anyway, to add a realistic touch of wear. If there are any flagstones left over, these can

22 The door between the gardener's room and the servants' hall creates the effect of rooms in use together. Garden produce can be brought in this way.

23 A flagstone floor is laid in the gardener's and handyman's quarters.

24 The floor in the servants' hall is stained to resemble old pine; it would not have been sanded and scrubbed regularly as it was in the kitchen where food was prepared and cooked.

be used to make hearths like the one in my servants' hall, or laid as garden paths.

I prefer not to use grout on floors but to butt them together, as was the usual practice in Georgian basements where the flagstones were laid directly onto earth. (This is why such basements are almost always damp, unless the floor has been 'tanked' in recent times, and they often have a distinctive smell rather like a church crypt.)

Non-opening doors

In both my basement rooms, and also in the entrance hall, I have fitted doors on to the back wall. These do not open, but are merely glued on to the walls. The one from the servants' hall is intended to suggest a passage out under a staircase to the rooms above, while the double doors in the gardener's room are wide enough for servants to take out ladders, the carriage, and in winter the children's sleigh. Produce from the garden would also be brought in this way, to deliver to the cook. The door at the rear of the entrance hall is also realistic, as there would always be a way through to service rooms beyond.

Doors in different sizes and styles are widely available and need only to be painted, given a door knob or handle and glued in place. To complete the realistic effect, add a door case made from thin moulding, and remember to mitre the corners at the top.

Doors between adjoining rooms

Doors leading directly from one room to another are not all that common in a dolls' house, where more often they open on to a staircase in between. If you have a doorway, as in this basement, fitting a door is worth the trouble of screwing in hinges and adding a door case, which may be cut from a suitable wooden moulding.

Take care when fitting different flooring in adjacent rooms that the door will clear both. If necessary, shave off some of the bottom edge of the door with a surform (scraper) before fitting. Fill any gap between the two floors with a strip of wood, painted to match the door or a wooden floor.

25 As in all the rooms of this house, the drawing room fireplace is fitted directly on to the wall. This allows plenty of space to place furniture on each side. A chimney breast would extend by 1–1½ in (25–38mm) on either side of the fireplace, taking up more wall space.

Chimney breasts

As you will see from the pictured rooms, I decided to omit chimney breasts in this house, and assume external flues, to allow more space inside and simplify decoration.

Fireplaces

The elaborate Adam-style fireplace in the dining room was bought ready-finished. For economy, use a fireplace made of inexpensive cast resin that can be painted. A marble effect is easy to achieve.

Method

1 Look at some pictures of real marble and see how the veins appear on your chosen specimen, then try a practice piece on card.

2 Use model enamel or satin-finish paint for the base coat; this might be off-white, cream or pale grey.

3 With a very fine brush, lightly feather in the veins and a few smudges in a suitable colour, based on your specimen picture. You may want to use a third colour, either a lighter or darker tone of the same contrast shade to give a realistic effect.

26 Two different styles of Georgian fireplace to choose from. For comparison, the Victorian version with round-headed opening shows the finish before painting. The other two have been painted as marble to suit planned schemes of decoration.

To make a surround for a grate use dark grey card, which will give a better effect than stark black. Cut the card slightly larger than the grate aperture and glue it directly on to the wall before fitting the fireplace on top. The hearths in this house are cut from samples of marbled card to tone with the painted finish on each fireplace. The exception is in the servants' hall, where I used two left-over flagstones, cut to fit.

The fittings

Georgian-style skirtings and cornices have been fitted throughout this house. I omitted dado rails as I wanted to make the most of the wallpapers by using them over the full height of the walls. Dado rails should only be fitted if you plan to paint below them and paper above.

The decorations

Choose paint colours that might have been used at the imagined date of your house. Ranges of historic paint shades from modern manufacturers always include a Georgian white: these will vary, but as long as you use an off-white and not a modern, brilliant white paint, the effect should be fine.

For servants' rooms, the paintwork was more likely to be a colour called drab or mouse, a dull fawn or grey-green. In fact, you can choose any beige-grey or soft grey-green.

Note that all paints were matt, never glossy. A satin finish in the family rooms will create a light-reflecting effect, but water-based matt paint can be used in the plainer servants' rooms, as in the basement and kitchen of this house.

Wallpapers

Choosing wallpapers is an enjoyable task; there are so many delightful 1:12 scale wallpapers, many based on historic patterns, that it may take longer than you expect. Do not be frightened by a bold design – many 19th-century wallpapers had vivid colours and interesting patterns. Just ensure that when the house is opened there are no violent colour clashes – try to arrange a scheme where the rooms present a coordinated effect.

27 The completed decorations are colour coordinated so that there are no jarring notes.

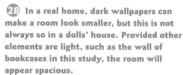

28 In a real home, dark wallpapers can make a room look smaller, but this is not always so in a dolls' house. Provided other elements are light, such as the wall of bookcases in this study, the room will appear spacious.

29 In general, people spend less time in a dining room than elsewhere in the home, so a bold pattern in a rich colour can be used. The ready-made Adam-style fireplace has a green 'marble' surround that reinforces the colour scheme.

30 Pretty flower prints were just coming into fashion and were used in bedrooms. The nursery fireplace, with its carved detail, is painted to simulate wood rather than marble to give a simple look.

The furniture

This dolls' house, like all my houses, contains a mixture of commissioned and ready-made furniture, as well as pieces that have been assembled from kits and some inexpensive whitewood furniture that has been painted to suit the room schemes.

Although it is possible to make simple furniture (see examples in the Heal's conversion on page 37), achieving the minute detail and complexity of the finest Georgian furniture will be beyond the skill of all but the most gifted amateurs.

Good-quality furniture is available from dolls' house shops and regular mail order ranges, but it is worth saving up for some pieces made by miniaturists whose speciality is Georgian-style furniture, and which will give you lasting pleasure. All the examples opposite are in my Georgian house. They were bought over a period of years – some were made to order and were well worth waiting for.

31 The small size of a davenport desk made it useful to fit into a corner of a room. It was considered a lady's desk; the many drawers were useful for her receipts and correspondence.

32 A side table with a 'marble' top and cabriole legs provides a good first impression in the hall. This design dates from around 1750, so was presumably inherited by the family. On top, the handmade lion is sculpted and cast in bronze.

33 In marked contrast to the couch used as a day bed, this wide armchair, dating from the end of the Regency period, has turned legs which anticipate Victorian designs.

34 In the family rooms, furniture was less formal; this yew wood chest of drawers has many uses. On top, a Staffordshire figure of a shepherd and a sheep and a personalized, two-handled loving cup add to the effect of well-loved family pieces.

35 Tub chairs were a Georgian style that is perhaps better known to us today through their reappearance during the 1920s and 30s. They were, and still are, often used in a study or library.

36 Irish Georgian furniture and accessories are often even more magnificent than English pieces. A turf bucket by the fireside is more elegant than a coal-scuttle!

37 An elegant Regency couch with sabre legs is enhanced by delicate carving. The striped silk covering in mid-green would have been a fashionable choice.

38 A small occasional table with barley-sugar twist legs may be used as a bedside table. The glass chamber candlestick holds a removable glass candle, neatly solving the problem of finding a candle to fit.

39 Neoclassical furniture designs became popular during the 18th century. This simple, elegant side table shows off the beauty of the yew from which this miniature is made. Side tables could be used to display a floral arrangement or, as here, a sculptural group on a marble base.

Painted furniture

A few pieces of painted furniture will add colour and will be useful in kitchens, bedrooms and nurseries. Whitewood furniture is generally inexpensive and has a clean, smooth surface that needs little sanding before painting with acrylic paint to give it a pretty effect.

Stained furniture

The impressive table in the library is also of whitewood, stained and polished to resemble mahogany. This is a very inexpensive table; always sand such pieces very carefully, because if there are any minute traces of the manufacturer's glue on the surface, the stain will not take. Apply mahogany wood stain with a clean cloth.

On any carved areas, use a paintbrush or cotton bud and work the stain well in.

T I P

If, after all your care, you find that there are still small patches where the stain has not taken, all is not lost. Sand these parts again, then use a dark brown felt-tip pen to cover them, working the colour in as far as possible. Finally, polish with dark brown shoe polish, then use this as a final polish all over the piece.

40 A striking colour choice for a set of shelves; the whitewood is painted with deep ochre acrylic to show off a collection of blue-and-white china in the kitchen.

41 The table before its transformation.

42 Mahogany wood dye and plenty of polish transform this inexpensive table so that it can be used in a library.

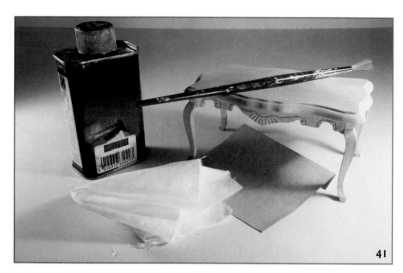

41

40

42

Assemble Georgian furniture from kits

I made up two furniture kits to add further interest to the nursery, where they would certainly have been in use at the time. They are made of mahogany, the favoured wood in the Georgian period. It does not need to be stained before polishing to give a good finish. See 'Furniture for your dolls' house' on pages 167–169 for further examples and guidance on furniture kit assembly.

This Georgian house is the largest I have ever assembled from a kit: I enjoyed the experience and am delighted with the completed house.

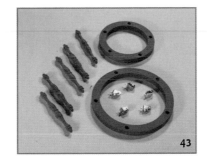
43

44

For me, it has the added attraction of being based on a typical house in Bath; I could include many details from houses I see and go inside often, as many are still in use as museums and also restaurants, with most of the interiors restored. From these visits and from reading local history, I am confident that

the furnishings are correct and I have a good idea of the lifestyle of the supposed inhabitants of my dolls' house.

I now realise that if you can choose a dolls' house with some connection to your own locality, you can personalize it through knowledge of local past events and in a style you are familiar with, to give it a very special ambience.

45

46

43 44 A baby walker was in use before the invention of the playpen, to keep toddlers safe and to help them to learn to walk. This nice example, shown with the parts to assemble it, has brass castors.

45 46 A counting frame would keep small children usefully occupied. This mahogany example is made from a simple kit that includes tiny beads to thread onto wire. It is as easy to complete as counting from one to ten.

47 I can imagine the heroine of a Georgette Heyer novel being taken for a drive in some comfort in this frivolous-looking carriage, with its leather-buttoned seat and scalloped canopy to protect her from the weather.

47

Chapter 5
Georgian mansion

This magnificent Georgian mansion was designed, built and decorated by two hobbyists who had never before tackled such a project. It has taken seven years to complete, an on-going labour of love that will continue as a retirement hobby with the gradual accumulation of more furniture and accessories.

It is a demonstration of what can be achieved with enthusiasm, dedication and patience, and although few of us would want to tackle such a mammoth project, it will provide inspiration to anyone building their own dolls' house.

How did the project begin?

Maria and Charles Nowakowska had never considered dolls' houses and miniatures as a hobby until they retired from their commercial photography business in autumn 2000. But shortly afterwards, they came across a dolls' house shop, went in out of curiosity, and were enchanted. They visited other dolls' house shops and exhibitions in their locality and then they went to Miniatura, the largest dolls' house fair in Britain. 'It opened our eyes to the quality and fine workmanship of craftsmen and women all over the world,' said Maria.

Big ideas

After much discussion, the new hobbyists decided that they wanted a house of larger dimensions than the average dolls' house, and that they would design and build it themselves. It helped that Charles is an experienced woodworker and

1 The magnificent façade of the dolls' house mansion; a street scene is planned in front of the railings.

2 A visitor ascends the entrance steps.

3 The completed interior shown from the front of the house.

4 The first part of the house is completed. In the background the second, larger, section takes shape.

5 A side view of the main part of the house, with its tented veranda. Further schemes for the garden are planned.

electrician, for without his skills in cutting out the MDF (medium density fibreboard) and installing the wiring for the lights, the house could never have been made.

Maria had a vision of her dream dolls' house, inspired by visits to the Palace of Versailles, the Doge's Palace in Venice, and seeing films showing the interiors of Windsor Castle and Buckingham Palace. She also wanted the opportunity to try out gilding, fine sewing and lavish decorations small-scale, and fill their creation with the best craftsman-made furniture and accessories.

'I had so many ideas that only a really large house would do, and as a retirement project, I had time at my disposal,' Maria explained. When they saw miniature versions of palaces made by Mulvany and Rogers and the Modelroom, they decided to see if they could achieve a similar lavish style in 1:12 scale.

6

Making plans

The planning stage was lengthy.
They began relatively modestly,
with Maria drawing out designs for
a house of two main floors and an
attic, with a terrace running the full
length at the back. At first this was
intended to be the full extent of
their project, as this section alone
has fourteen rooms.

Although always interested in home
decoration and garden design, Maria
had no training as a draughtsperson.
She worked out the number of walls
and floors that could be cut from a
sheet of MDF measuring 8 x 4ft
(2440 x 1220mm) and made her
plans accordingly. Next she drew out
the walls and floors directly on to
the MDF, so that Charles could cut
out the pieces. It was a practical

method that worked well, and soon
they began to build, tackling the
assembly together.

Sensibly, they had decided to
construct each floor as a stand-alone
section, to include floor, ceiling,
walls and the electric wiring and
lighting for that section. This
arrangement meant that Charles
could install individual lighting
circuits for each floor. He used 253
light bulbs to create a dazzling
display which would show off
the lavish interiors by the time
the house was completed.

Larger plans

As she planned the rooms, Maria's
ideas went a stage further; eventually
Charles and Maria made a joint
decision that this first part of the

6 The main staircase rises from the
entrance hall through two floors and
extends above to link up with the
upper section that will be added later.

7 The rich gilding in the magnificent
library is enhanced by the use of mirrors
on the back wall, which reflect the
lighting and create a perspective effect.

8 When not entertaining in the grand
reception rooms, the family use their
private parlour, which is comfortably
furnished with a set of brocade-covered
chairs. Elegant French windows lead on
to the terrace.

house would become the upper part
of a radically larger mansion. The
additional four storeys that followed
to form the lower part of the house
are more spacious, allowing for the
grand reception rooms, while the
first-built section is used for family
bedrooms and children's nurseries
and playrooms.

Working from top to bottom

Maria cheerfully admits that building the upper storeys first is hardly the accepted way to go

9 The main bedroom has space for a sofa, a day-bed and a four-poster bed.

10 Maria made the bed hangings and bedspread in fine silk to tone with the bedroom colour scheme.

11 In the servants' part of the house, a small area has been set aside for ironing and sewing, and a water closet is tucked away under the stairs.

about things, as it is generally best to plan out the entire scheme at the beginning. But with a house of this size it would have been impossible to build it all in one piece without standing perilously on step-ladders in order to decorate the upper rooms.

They also learned from early miscalculations: Maria wanted to include gilded plasterwork on ceilings, but soon realised that these would not be seen clearly unless some of the rooms were higher.

Initially she had chosen a standard height for the ceiling of 10–10½in (255–270mm), but in the second part to be built, containing the main reception rooms, the ceilings are

12 13 The dining room extends from front to back of the house and it is the most lavishly decorated part of the mansion. It includes marbled columns and fireplaces, gilded furniture, picture frames and mirrors. The twelve dining chairs are set around a long table which is covered by a handmade tablecloth. There is a complete dinner service for twelve, together with silver serving dishes and other tableware. Chandeliers hang from the gilded ceiling and the walls are covered in French silk.

12in (305mm) and even 14in (355mm) high in the largest rooms. This allows for chandeliers and tall windows so that she could indulge her love of fine needlework and provide elaborate curtain treatments.

It also makes the mansion more architecturally correct, since the entrance hall and reception rooms in a Georgian house were designed to impress, with high ceilings and lavish decoration.

14 Conveniently placed for after-dinner entertainment, the music room is flanked by a pillared corridor at the side. The needlepoint rug was hand-worked.

The dolls' house got larger

The scale of the house is astonishing. The completed mansion of seven floors stands 7ft 5in (2.26m) high, 5ft 5in (1.65m) wide and 5ft (1.52m) deep. There are 30 rooms; seven staircases; 47 windows; 26 doors; ten balconies and ten window-guards; one terrace; three gardens and a grotto.

Best of all, it functions like a real house, with front and back rooms and corridors connecting with the staircases, so that in theory, it would be possible to walk from the cellar at the rear of the house, right up to the children's nursery in the attic.

15 The grotto is fitted in under the entrance steps that lead up to the front door. It is only glimpsed by looking along a corridor, providing a surprise feature.

16 The brick-floored cellar provides plenty of storage for wine and barrels of dried goods.

17 The corridor and back stairs are extremely realistic. The chequerboard floor tiles have been laid individually.

18 The array of blue-and-white china and copper pans in the kitchen is worthy of a stately home; a checked cotton tablecloth provides a coordinated colour accent.

19 The main staircase looks as impressive as Maria and Charles had hoped, but needed some adjustment for John to make and fit the balusters and handrail. Designing a staircase with a curve needs mathematical ability in order to ensure that balusters can be arranged symmetrically, and is not really a job for an amateur. The gilded M on the balustrade gives Maria great pleasure. The hand-painted marbling on the staircase and hall floor is all her work.

countless lengths of railings. He made railings to go alongside the entrance steps and provided two pillars. In addition, he completed the curving main staircase that had been designed and made by Maria and Charles, and painted as marble by Maria. Until they met John, they had wondered how they were to provide the staircase balusters and handrail, but finally this problem was solved and, to Maria's delight, John worked a letter M on the first landing as a final flourish.

A lived-in home

This Georgian mansion is supposedly lived in by a Victorian family, so that both Georgian and Victorian furniture could be included and placed as it might have been when in use. Exquisitely dressed dolls are also present in the rooms, because such a large house would almost certainly seem empty without any inhabitants to add that essential feeling of use. Maria thought very carefully about the furniture that they bought and commissioned so that it would suit their story. A few of their choices – and some other fine furniture that would fit in equally well in a mansion of this period style – are shown on the following pages.

Wrought ironwork

Maria and Charles live near to the Regency town of Cheltenham that is renowned for the quality and abundance of the wrought ironwork and later, cast ironwork, on so many of its elegant houses. They wanted their dolls' house to be finished with similar balconies and railings but were not sure how to achieve it.

Then they had a stroke of luck: they met John Watkins, master metalworker, who although allegedly retired had been invited to show once more at Miniatura as a special guest. It turned out that he did not

live far away, and they invited him to see their unfinished dolls' house. John was impressed, so much so that he agreed to make some balconies and railings – but as he explained to me, he had no idea when he started of exactly how much work this would entail.

By the time the house was completed, he had made the railings for ten balconies in the much-admired Heart and Honeysuckle pattern that features on many Regency houses. For the terrace and gardens, he made ten window-guards, two tented verandas, two pairs of gates and a single gate and

20 The principal rooms at the back of the mansion.

21 The gilded furniture in the dining room was made by a master miniaturist who has completed many rooms for the Guthrie Collection of Miniature Model Houses at Hever Castle, Kent.

22 This splendid writing desk is made in walnut with a green leather top.

23

26

24

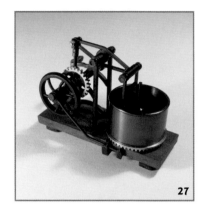

27

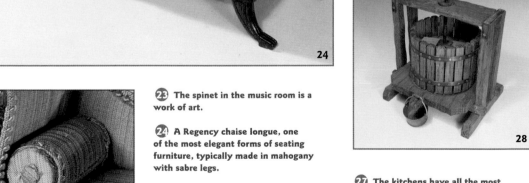

28

25

23 The spinet in the music room is a work of art.

24 A Regency chaise longue, one of the most elegant forms of seating furniture, typically made in mahogany with sabre legs.

25 A detail of the chaise longue, showing the masterly ropework carving.

26 A Queen Anne chair with buttoned leather upholstery would make a striking addition to any Georgian house.

27 The kitchens have all the most up-to-date equipment, including this early version of a food processor. The miniature is a working model.

28 A wine press might be considered an essential item for a cellar.

Design and build your own dolls' house

If you are inspired by Maria and Charles's achievements to build your own house, here is some guidance. With a kit house or a ready-made house, any potential problems will have been thought through and dealt with at the planning stage. If you design your own, you are bound to meet problems as you proceed that you may not have considered. I would not advise anyone to self-build a dolls' house unless they already have some woodwork experience – better to buy a ready-built dolls' house or assemble one from a kit, and concentrate your efforts on the decorations. But if you have sufficient experience, building a dolls' house can be very rewarding.

Here are some points to watch when working in miniature scale, that even the experienced woodworker may not have thought of before down-sizing.

Consider the expense
Plywood and MDF are both expensive to begin with, so size will affect the cost. Maria and Charles's house needed 11 sheets of 8 x 4ft (2440 x 1220mm) MDF to construct their mansion, but plywood would have cost far more.

When buying a ready-made house of even modest proportions, relatively few hobbyists pause to consider how much it will cost to decorate and furnish the rooms. Even if you make many of the contents yourself, the total can mount up alarmingly over time if you decide on a large house.

But if, like Maria and Charles, your plans get bigger, and you want to furnish your house with craftsman-made furniture and accessories, the total expenditure can run into a sizeable chunk of income. Just consider all this before you start.

Fixtures and fittings
Ready-made doors, window frames, architraves and balustrades are all available from suppliers of dolls' house fittings, in standard sizes to suit 1:12 at relatively modest cost, so there is no need to make your own.

Stair kits to assemble flights with ready-cut treads, balusters and newel posts will fit most regular sizes of dolls' houses. Plan carefully to ensure that you select major components that will fit your design.

29 **Work is in progress on this ready-made staircase.**

29

Cutting apertures for doors and windows

• The front door
The front door should open inward and needs clearance over flooring or carpeting in the entrance hall. One excellent method is to fit the front door over a small step on the outside, so that when it is opened, it will clear any flooring.

• Internal doors
Similarly, internal doors must allow clearance. Check this out carefully and, if possible, decide on the type of hard or soft flooring in advance. One useful method is to fit internal doors above ground level, and after fitting hard flooring or carpet, fill the gap between rooms (under the door) with a thin piece of stripwood to make the floors level. This works particularly well if you plan wooden plank flooring, because the strip can be of the same thickness and stained to match. Another method is to fit a length of thin brass strip (available in various widths from model shops) to represent the brass edging strip used in real-life homes. It is easy to cut and glue in place.

• Windows
Do not place window apertures too close to an opening front or too near to the floor level. Allow for clearance for window frames and sills. Also take into account that any curtains will take up extra space and must not catch.

30

Consider fitting a side or rear window. This is a nice feature that is not always offered on a ready-made dolls' house, mainly because it may make placing furniture difficult. The best place for such a window is on a landing.

Make decoration easy
Provide a removable panel at the back to gain access to stairs and landings. Fix the panel with screws into the ends of the walls on either side of the staircase so that it can be removed easily and replaced after internal decorations are completed.

Painting or papering around a fixed-in staircase with no back access can be very difficult. Fitting flooring on landings or stair carpet will also be simplified by having a removable wall panel.

31 A window on a landing is fitted with a neat, space-saving blind so that there will be enough room for a small table or plant in a jardinière to furnish the landing.

32 Decorating in a staircase well allows little room for manoeuvre.

33 Maria enjoyed gilding the decorative features and ceilings in the most important rooms of her house.

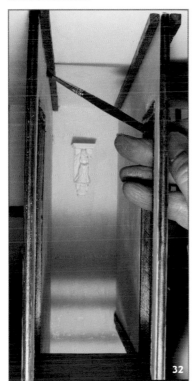

How will you move the house?
MDF is heavy and it can be difficult to carry even a moderate size of dolls' house. Consider fitting castors to the base if you will only want to move it from one room to another on the same floor level, or from an adjacent workshop. *Do not* attempt to pick up and move a dolls' house that you know to be heavy. If the house has to be moved from one floor level to another, I would recommend employing professional removal men.

Decorative detail
A grand house can be enhanced with decorative gilding, as seen in this mansion. Real gold leaf is very expensive and there are several economical alternatives. One option is imitation gold leaf. The method for applying it is as follows.

Method

1 Imitation gold leaf is available from stockists of artists' materials in a pack of thin sheets.

2 Application works best on a flat surface. Brush the surface over with gold size and leave for a couple of minutes so that it becomes tacky.

3 Lift up a sliver of the gold with tweezers, and brush it on gently with a soft brush.

There are a number of makes of brush-on liquid gold (and silver) that are easy to apply straight from the bottle. Follow the instructions carefully to get a good result.

Gold model enamel, applied carefully, will also look good. Do a test piece first to see how it works on different surfaces – paper, wood or plaster. Use a fine brush and make sure that you stir the enamel continually during application.

34 A gold pen can be used on narrow mouldings.

My own preferred method is to use a gold pen, the sort that has to be shaken before and during application. To avoid blots, I like to eject a small puddle on to a plastic lid from a jar, then dip the pen into that and apply. This method works well on narrow mouldings and is less messy than paint, as there is no need to clean brushes.

35 Gold braid makes a neat finish to the edge of the silk fabric covering the wall over an arched opening.

Attaching fabric to walls

For a really sumptuous effect, walls can be covered with fabric instead of wallpaper.

Method

1 Cut patterns in stiff paper, as for wallpaper, allowing ¼in (6mm) overlap at the back edges in the rooms. Then very carefully cut the fabric, using sharp scissors.

2 Apply spray mount to the walls and leave until tacky, then gently press on the fabric.

You will need to practise this method, to make sure that you know how much spray mount to apply and also how long to leave it. Too much can mark thin silks, so do not start this on your only piece of fabric.

Make covers for chairs

The same method can be used to fix chair seats and backs in your own choice of fabric.

Cut a pattern from tracing or greaseproof paper, which is thin enough to bend over the edges of the seat or chair back to check the fit, and proceed as for covering walls with fabric.

36 Maria made draped curtains with pelmets and tie-backs. In a formal room box pelmets work well, and the fabric can be mounted on card or wood. For tie-backs, use iron-on dressmakers' stiffening so that they keep their shape.

37 Something to aim for: a Queen Anne armchair, beautifully covered with fine needlepoint by a professional miniaturist.

38 A detail of the fine needlepoint used to cover the chair.

TIP

It can be difficult to find fine enough braid to edge the upholstery. Make your own by twisting together single strands of embroidery silk, adding a dab of glue at intervals to keep it in place.

36

37

38

39 To adapt a clean whitewood sink unit to use in a Victorian scullery, use wood stain. After applying, and before the stain is dry, rub off parts to show wear.

A set of library steps is invaluable in the Georgian study or library, where shelves were often up to ceiling height.

The corner chair to assemble from a whitewood kit is another interesting piece. It is based on similar examples from the late 18th and early 19th centuries, copied by country chair-makers with some knowledge of Chippendale's pattern books, or even a chair-maker who had not seen the pattern books but had heard the patterns described. The back splats owe something to Chippendale, but the cresting is typical of a type of Windsor chair known as a smoker's bow.

The furniture

The mansion is furnished almost entirely with miniatures made by the leading makers working today. But you can paint your own furniture, and some assembled from kits might make a welcome (and less expensive) addition to even the grandest house. Here are two furniture kits to assemble.

40 A set of library steps can be assembled from a kit. Here the pieces are laid out ready to put together.

The chair looks comfortable and would provide ample seating for a substantial person: it might be useful in a butler's or upper servant's room. Similar chairs came to be known as 'country Chippendale' and were much used in the homes of farmers, who liked pieces of good, solid English furniture. The originals were usually made of elm and oak.

Maria and Charles's house will become a family heirloom. 'It is a lifetime project, which may never be completely finished, but every minute is enjoyable,' says Maria. And already her young granddaughter is taking an interest, so the future of the dolls' house mansion seems guaranteed.

41 The completed steps are a good reproduction of full-size versions, always made in mahogany, like the kit.

42 This corner chair is made from whitewood, which has then been stained and polished. The fabric to cover the seat is provided with the kit.

43 The whitewood parts to assemble the corner chair kit.

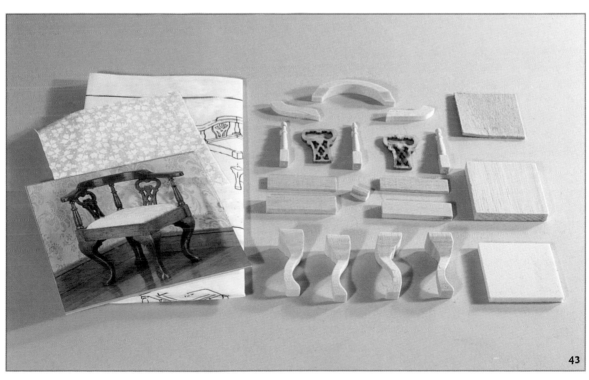

Chapter 6
Regency Gothic folly

The Georgian period spanned the reigns of the first four King Georges of England, from 1714 to 1830. The house and the mansion in the previous two chapters are both stylistically from this period. But there was a curious blip in the classical ideas at the beginning of the 19th century.

① A Gothic folly makes an unusual dolls' house project. Any dolls' house castle can be decorated in 19th-century Gothic style rather than as a more typical medieval fortress.

In 1811 the Prince Regent, who was later to become King George IV, was given responsibility as Head of State during his father's prolonged bouts of illness. The Prince was extravagant and led a hedonistic lifestyle, but he had a good knowledge of art and architecture, and his ideas were copied. Then, as now, people enjoyed trying out new interior decorations, and there was a growing interest in oriental styles.

It was at this time that the Gothic Revival movement began, initially through the example of Sir Horace Walpole, whose extraordinary Gothic fantasy, Strawberry Hill, inspired many gentlemen to redecorate at least part of their stately homes in the newly fashionable style.

Gothic style

Gothic style – or Gothick as it is sometimes written, to distinguish the revivalist style from the original Gothic of the 13th century – is dramatic. Features include windows with stone tracery, and sometimes stained glass, elaborately plastered or painted ceilings, spiral stone staircases and decorative cornices and fireplaces, all enhanced by the use of rich colours on the walls.

A Regency folly

This splendid 1:12 Gothic tower is supplied as a ready-built shell. Although it is not a kit, there are many fixtures and fittings for the hobbyist to put in place, so that completing and decorating the tower gives a real feeling of satisfaction.

② Interior lighting provides a tantalizing glimpse of the rooms inside through the open door and the delicate tracery of the window.

3 There are plenty of Gothic features to add to complete the tower.

4 Window frames and pinnacles are made of cast resin in a warm terracotta that can be painted as stone if preferred.

5 The flat roof is fitted with a (non-opening) trapdoor to suggest a route for access.

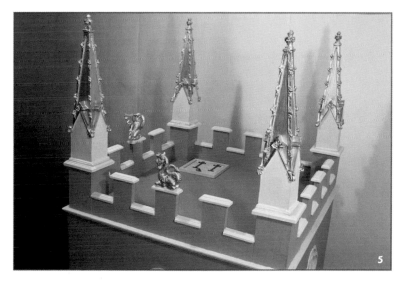

The stairs are left free to aid interior decoration. The Gothic window frames are of cast resin, to slot and glue into place after decorating the exterior. The main porch and front door, with columns and a castellated balcony, the roof with pinnacles at each corner and even two carved, heraldic beasts to fit on top, are all separate pieces.

Like other dolls' houses resembling medieval castles, the tower could be completed with grey, rough-cast walls and a medieval interior. However, I decided to choose the Regency Gothic style inspired by a local landmark, Beckford's Tower, which still stands on top of a hill at Lansdown, near Bath, England.

It was built by wealthy connoisseur William Beckford and is in classical Italianate style, but this was his second attempt at tower-building his first, in the Gothic style, sadly collapsed. The Lansdown tower is topped by a lantern that astonishes everyone who sees it, gilded with real gold leaf that glows in the sun. A lantern is available as an optional extra for the dolls' house tower, and for me this was the deciding factor.

The exterior decoration

In order to make the folly as striking as possible, I chose a rich, deep pink water-based paint for the walls. Generally I use satin-finish paint on the outside of dolls' houses, but this has a matt finish to look and feel more like colour-washed stone. A textured paint could be used as an alternative, for a rough-cast look.

The window frames, porch and architectural details are painted as stone for contrast, while for the front door, I mixed a streaky grey-white to mimic the colour of ancient oak.

The windows

Stained glass was enjoying a revival during the Regency. Only one set of window frames is supplied as standard with this dolls' house, but an extra set can be ordered to fit inside, so that glazing can be sandwiched in between.

The realistic stained-glass effect is reproduced by using purple, mauve and clear acetate glazing (from a supplier of artists' materials), glued on to the inner edge of the outer window frames before these are fixed in place. The joins between coloured and clear glazing on the long windows are covered up by the horizontal glazing bars.

6 Like William Beckford, I wanted the folly to be a real show-stopper; as well as gilding the pinnacles I also added some frilly Gothic mouldings to the top of the lantern. I used gold model enamel for all the gilding.

7 Two heraldic beasts, ready to gild and place on the castellated parapet.

Fitting the glazing and the inner windows required some perseverance but the effect was well worth the effort. My method involved cutting patterns for each window in tracing paper, then transferring the shape to coloured or clear acetate and checking for an exact fit. Each piece was carefully glued in place with a minuscule amount of PVA glue, applied with a cocktail stick around the outer edges. Lastly, the inner frame was fitted on top; ensure you take care not to smear any glue on to the glazing.

The acetate can be cut and laid aside with the window frames, to be fitted after completing the interior decorations.

8 Coloured glazing reflects into the rooms to produce a constantly changing effect according to the light outside.

TIP

The standard method of wallpapering over walls with windows is to paper over the entire wall, and when thoroughly dried out, cut out the apertures with a sharp craft knife. This is essential when dealing with oddly shaped windows such as the ones here.

9 A glimpse of the rooms inside the castle. The interior window frames add a realistic touch to the otherwise plain front.

The interior

Aim to impress when decorating the interior of a folly; a connoisseur like Beckford would want to amaze his guests. Features such as deep-toned wallpapers, gilding and plasterwork, marble and granite flooring can all be included.

Fitting the staircase

The curving spiral staircase resembles the one in Beckford's real tower; although that rises to 120ft (36.6m), it has exceptionally shallow, wide treads, and is so well-designed that reaching the top feels like climbing a gentle slope.

10

The dolls' house is supplied with the staircase already in place, but not fixed in – they are a close fit in the stairwell.

Taking stairs out and putting them back is something you may need to do when decorating many dolls' houses constructed from kits, but it is not always possible with a ready-made and fully finished house if the maker has fixed them in place. In this case, I found it convenient to remove them while I decorated the stairwell and the adjacent area and fitted the floors.

The following method explains how to remove and replace the stairs in this house. It works with most staircases that are obviously not glued in place but which at first sight may appear immovable.

Method

1 Take out the lower flight first. Push upwards firmly, tilt the base towards yourself and pull the lower end out first. Follow the same procedure for the top flight – you may have to push upwards quite hard, as they are a very tight fit.

2 To put the stairs back, reverse the procedure – top flight first, then lower flight. Angle in the top flight, push up through the opening, then slide the base into place so that it is flush with the upper floor.

10 Based on a tower built by an eccentric owner with an eye for striking decorations, wallpapers are in the rich tones he favoured, and picked out in gold. Together with the plaster mouldings, this creates a splendid impression.

11 Wallpapers, ceiling papers and flooring are from a variety of sources: none are regular dolls' house wallpapers.

Method

1 Fit the stairs in place temporarily and mark the zigzag lower edge of the treads in pencil on the wall.

2 Take out the stairs and draw a straight line ½in (12mm) above the marking. Paint above this line, then wallpaper below it so that the join will be concealed when you fit the stairs in permanently.

3 Note that the bedroom wallpaper can extend across the back wall above the stairwell. Fit a thin moulding as a divider between paper and the painted wall below.

3 Put the top of the lower flight into the opening, then swing the stairs back against the wall.

I have gone into some detail on this procedure because it took me some time to work out what to do. Hopefully if you, too, have this particular house you will be able to deal with the stairs without even thinking about it!

Achieve a neat join between two different decorative treatments adjacent to a stairwell, like this one, with the following procedure.

12 Paint the stairs to resemble stone (matt stone model enamel will give a good finish) before final fitting. Remember to paint the undersides of the treads of the top flight, which will be visible from below. This will also apply to any spiral staircase that is not boxed in.

Plaster mouldings

Throughout the tower I used plaster mouldings, fireplaces and bookcases in a consistently Gothic style.

Cutting plaster mouldings is no more difficult than cutting wooden ones. Use a mini mitre box for both angled and straight cuts, and a very fine razor saw blade – 52 teeth per inch (25mm) works well and most hobby shops will have these in stock to fit into your regular saw handle.

To balance my extravagant spending on plasterwork, I economized by using fancy stripwood from a hardware store, painted a stone colour to look like stone skirtings. I also used decorative art papers,

13 The fireplace in the entrance hall is a welcoming sight to greet visitors, while the coat of arms above (a copy in reduced size of one largely invented by Beckford) is designed to impress.

14 The entrance hall doubles as a classical sculpture gallery, with columns and wall brackets supporting statues and busts. The extravagant Gothic-style mouldings are set off by the deep pink on the walls, a colour that was used on the staircase of the Lansdown tower.

samples of regular wallpapers and giftwrap as wall and ceiling papers and to simulate granite, marble and tiled flooring. My well-tried method is to use paper templates for cutting the wallpapers and card patterns to fit the floors. Flooring paper can be glued to the card before fixing the floor in place with pieces of double-sided Scotch tape.

The drawing room

The drawing room reflects Beckford's taste in furnishings as well as his intellectual pursuits. No gentleman's study or library would have been complete without a globe, so I have provided one here. This fanciful version is made from crystal. There is also a microscope in the room for scientific study.

Although all the other rooms in the tower are uncurtained to show off the windows, Beckford did have curtains in his own drawing room.

15 The red-and-grey mottled art paper used as flooring is similar to a granite chosen by Beckford. The gilt chairs are Christmas decorations: they are slightly smaller in scale, but arranged in the window embrasure, they make an attractive group.

16 On the other side of the drawing room, my collection of ebony woodturnings looks suitably Gothic in the bookcase.

17 A painting of Beckford's family home, Fonthill Abbey, hangs above the fireplace. The abbey is shown before he added a 300ft (90m) Gothic tower.

18 The curtains look suitably opulent.

19 Heraldic crests on the flooring and a gilded initial 'B' on the wall personalize the bedroom.

I decided to create an elaborate window treatment, based on the arrangements shown in *Ackermann's Repository*, the Regency decorator's style guide.

I used silk ribbon, braid and looped gold edging, mounted on a thin card base, cut to surround the window. It took me most of a day to achieve something I felt Beckford would have approved. Once completed, it was easy to attach the whole arrangement to the wall using adhesive putty.

The bedroom

There is no record of a bedroom in Beckford's Tower, which was built solely for the purpose of housing his art collection and to use for study. To complete the folly as a dolls' house, I created an imaginary bedroom. For an extra touch of fantasy, I based it on the designs of the equally eccentric William Burgess for a bedroom at Castel Coch in Wales, which is of roughly the same period.

The bedroom ceiling is papered with a deep blue giftwrap sprinkled with stars to accentuate the effect of the toning art paper with a hint of silver used on the walls.

The bedroom can be used for study as well as sleeping because there is a well-filled bookcase and a comfortable sofa.

The furniture

Regency furniture was distinctive, often influenced by Indian or even Egyptian styles, following the lead of the Prince Regent. Gilding proliferated, and unusual feet in the shape of animal hooves on chairs and tables carried through these themes, while more classic pieces with sabre legs ending in gilded castors were also admired.

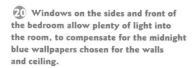 Windows on the sides and front of the bedroom allow plenty of light into the room, to compensate for the midnight blue wallpapers chosen for the walls and ceiling.

㉑ The painting above the bedroom fireplace shows Fonthill Abbey in all its glory, complete with the tower before it collapsed.

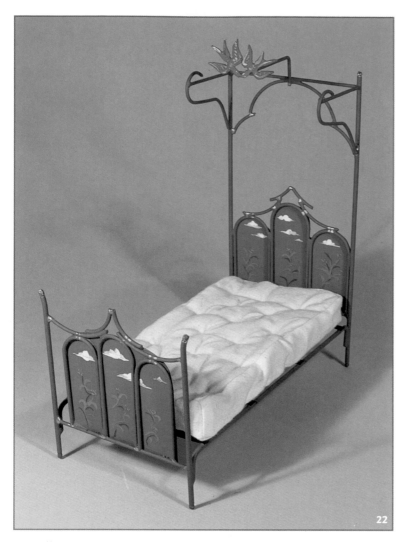

22 A handpainted metal bed with a canopy is a flight of fancy by a miniaturist who enjoys using his skills to make each piece of furniture unique.

23 A 'stone' table with a pedestal base that features a pair of swans is intended for use in a garden, but is suitable in a room with a bookcase of architectural design that also simulates stone.

24 A handsome collector's cabinet that needs a large room to show it off. It is available in walnut or mahogany, richly finished in gold or silver. It has 56 drawers, all of which can be opened. It is fitted out to take writing materials and ephemera such as drawings.

25 A detail of the cabinet partly closed shows the thickness of the front that contains the drawers. Remarkably, this impressive piece is from an inexpensive range of furniture.

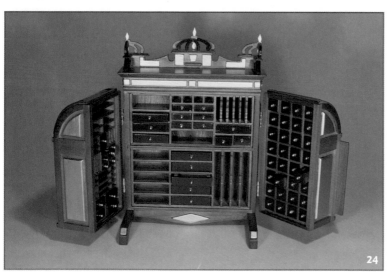

26 A side table and chair made in metal in simulation of painted bamboo. The very decorative finish is picked out in gold, while the faux marble table top is also handpainted.

27 28 The faux bamboo sofa and armchair, with its rich green silk upholstery, is characteristic of the late Regency period.

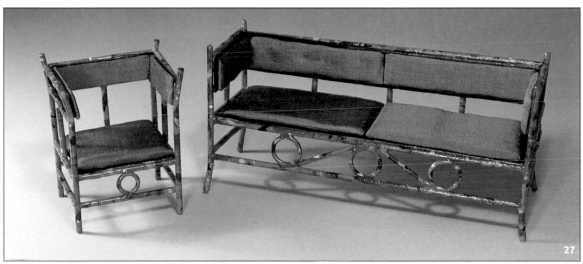

Fortunately, there is a wide choice of plainer furniture available in dolls' house shops. More unusual pieces, made by individual miniaturists, can often be repeated to order.

The ready-made pieces shown on these pages would suit a Regency dolls' house decorated in Gothic style. Faux bamboo furniture in imitation of Chinese style was widely admired, either in a natural-looking colour tinged with green, or in red or black picked out with gold.

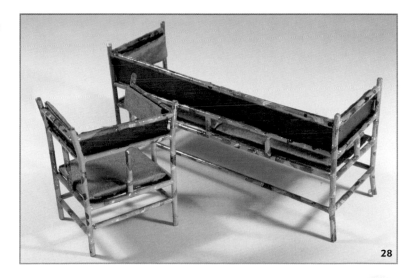

Painted furniture

Painted furniture was not a feature of most Regency rooms, where mahogany or satinwood with gilt fittings was preferred. But Chinese lacquer – or its English equivalent, 'japanned' furniture in chinoiserie style – appeared on cupboards, chests and even beds. In general, this treatment, too, is best left to professional miniaturists.

Assemble furniture from a kit

A decorative floor-standing mirror with a useful drawer in the base (taken from a design by Thomas Chippendale, furniture-maker to the aristocracy) is available as a kit. It resembles furniture made by Chippendale for a bedroom at Nostell Priory in Yorkshire, England, which was finished in green with gold chinoiserie decoration.

 **Exquisitely painted in chinoiserie by a professional miniaturist, this special chest-on-chest can be made to order.**

29

30

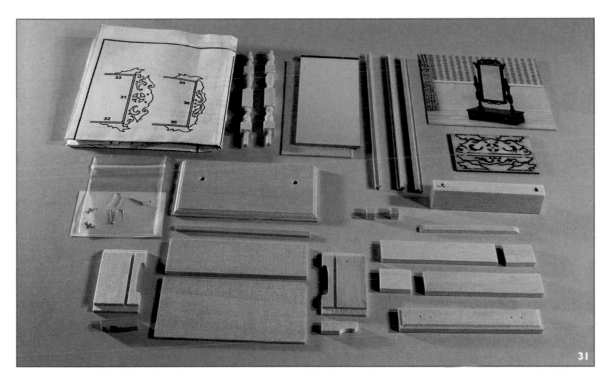

I chose to paint the mirror in a similar shade of green to that originally used by Chippendale (the pieces can still be seen in situ but the green is now faded to a greeny-yellow). Rather than attempt the chinoiserie decoration, I used a fineline gold pen to add finishing touches that were easier to achieve.

Regency innovations

Although I have used a specific dolls' house as my example, the decorative ideas would suit any Regency-style dolls' house or folly that might benefit from a touch of Gothic style.

The Regency period was a time when wealthy home-owners wanted to decorate their rooms in new and innovative ways, and they often got into debt to keep up with the latest trends. The Prince Regent set a bad example in this respect and he frequently had to ask Parliament to bail him out. His most expensive folly, the Royal Pavilion, in

Brighton, England, at first regarded with scepticism, did influence fashionable decor for many years. Anyone fortunate enough to visit it today can only marvel at its lavish interior.

A more sedate approach to decoration was, needless to say, favoured by the majority, but a touch of Gothic will liven up a conventional Regency room and indicate that the inhabitants of your dolls' house are aware of newly fashionable decoration and furnishing styles.

31 The parts to assemble a Chippendale-style mirror.

32 The completed mirror.

Chapter 7
Gothic cottage

This project is based on a ready-built Gothic two-room cottage, with a Cotswold-style Arts & Crafts interior. The 19th-century obsession with Gothic style was not confined to the large home. It was used even on small houses and lodges for the tenants on country estates.

The distinctive arched windows and doorways, derived from medieval style, were thought of as picturesque. When already existing cottages needed repairs, windows were often modified to echo the shape of those on the nearby grand house. In the UK, many pretty estate cottages that were Gothicized in this way are still in use today – sometimes with thatched roofs to add to their charm.

The Cotswolds, famous for the beauty of the creamy-yellow local stone that was used for building, became the centre of the Arts & Crafts movement. William Morris, often thought of as the man who began it all by his insistence on handwork and traditional skills, had his country home there. Many craftsmen followed his lead, and left London to set up workshops in the countryside – a tenet of the movement was that a simple life and closeness to nature were essential to the ideal existence.

One of them was renowned architect and silversmith C.R. Ashbee, who set up a Guild of Handicrafts in Chipping Campden, with the aim that its members would share an idyllic lifestyle, working and spending their leisure time together.

The Guild survived for twenty years, but was not a complete success, as it was difficult to sell work when so far from London.

A new use for a cottage

This ready-made, undecorated dolls' house is a nice example of a two-room Gothicized cottage; the rooms are large, with high ceilings, and I felt that it would be ideal to

2 William Morris instigated a revival of tapestry and needlepoint, and produced charts for amateur needlewomen to follow – the forerunners of the 'tapestry' kits we know today. This example was worked by a professional miniaturist who also provides kits to work on thread counts from 34 holes per inch (25mm) for the beginner to 54 holes per inch (25mm) for the experienced needleworker.

1 An attractive dolls' house with Gothicized windows and door, finished with a castellated roof. It is based on an estate cottage. The exterior is painted with satin-finish paint.

3 The planked front door, stained as oak, is set into a carved surround painted as stone. Burnished metal Gothic-style hinges and a ring handle, and lanterns on either side, complete the deliberately archaic effect.

All three were qualified architects who preferred to provide their own furniture designs for the houses that they built.

Daneway House, leased from Lord Bathurst, was originally quite grand: the old photograph that I saw in a book shows a stone floor, a massive manorial fireplace and a plasterwork ceiling, providing an interesting contrast with the plain but beautifully made furniture inside.

An Arts & Crafts interior can be arranged in a cottage, in an Edwardian house, or in a larger, more modern dolls' house. The style appealed to a cross-section of the public, and could be found in manor houses or suburban homes right up to the 1930s.

The interior of the cottage

The front door opens into the main room, with a staircase in the corner leading to the upper floor. The traces of 17th-century decorations hint at a grander past than the simple estate cottage – perhaps it had once been a dower house.

I was fortunate enough to have a large collection of Arts & Crafts miniature furniture and accessories. Always popular with professional miniaturists, similar furniture is available to buy these days both ready-made and in kit form.

4 The inside opening front is wallpapered, using a full-size design that features heraldic crests, to give an impression of earlier decorations.

house a collection of miniatures based on Arts & Crafts designs. These include furniture, pewter, woodturnings and pottery, suggesting that the former estate cottage has now been taken over by a group of craftworkers as a home for one of them as well as offering a sales outlet for their work.

This use was inspired by an old photograph showing a room at Daneway House, in the Cotswolds, that was used as a showroom by distinguished furniture-makers Ernest Gimson and the brothers Sidney and Ernest Barnsley.

5 An impressive 'stone' fireplace, in keeping with the supposed origins of this estate cottage, is an inexpensive piece made of cast resin.

6 Supper is ready – a simple meal of bread, cheese and cider, to be served on rustic pottery. The table, in the style of Voysey, has distinctive heart-shaped cut-outs on the supports, a motif to which he returned many times.

7 The living room that is also used as a showroom for furniture, pottery and woodturned objects.

8 The upstairs room is also a bedroom for one of the craftworkers. The simple furniture is all suited to the Arts & Crafts period. The bed is a copy of a design by Heal's of London, which appeared in an early catalogue as an example of 'cottage-style' furniture. Above it hangs a painting by naive artist Alfred Wallis, reduced in size from a picture in an art brochure and framed in plain, unvarnished wood.

9 The simple chest, fitted with a single drawer at the base, is typical of well-made Cotswold-style furniture. The Art Deco studio pottery above it continues the craft theme. A collection of woodturned tankards and some larger goblets are displayed on the chest.

10 The wives of Arts & Crafts workers generally confined their craft work to embroidery, weaving or basketmaking. Following their example, the patchwork quilt on the bed is also handmade and the rug on the floor is handwoven, both by professional miniaturists

11 A corner of the living room, with an oak Cotswold-style dresser loaded with country pottery, and with a place under the stairs for the baskets that were also made in the district.

Flooring

Whatever the exterior style of your dolls' house, there are particular interior features that you will need if you plan an Arts & Crafts setting. If it is a Cotswold cottage you will need a stone floor, and plain planked floors for upstairs rooms, perhaps softened by handwoven rugs.

Stone flooring

You can make your own floor in imitation of stone flags by several methods (see pages 16–17 for Tudor style and page 50 for a Georgian house). But in the main room of the cottage I used an effective method that is economical on a large floor.

Method

1 Use art board. This is available from shops that stock artists' materials. Buy it in A2 sheets (500 x 700mm).

2 Mark out and score irregular shapes to represent the stone slabs, using a craft knife and raised-edge metal ruler. Be careful not to cut right through the board.

3 Paint with matt paint in a stone colour. I used a water-based paint mixed with a little model enamel. Add a few patches in a darker shade to show wear and dirt and rub over with a dry cloth to blur the edges of the darker colour.

4 Glue the floor in place with PVA adhesive and finish with a coat of matt, acrylic varnish to protect the painted card surface from damage.

A wooden floor

To suit an updated cottage, the wooden planked floor should have a handmade look.

Method

1 Use wood strip, cut and fitted to give an uneven, worn effect, as for the Tudor planked floor on page 17. Finish with one coat of medium oak wood stain, plus one coat of satin varnish to give a polished but not over-shiny appearance.

2 For an Arts & Crafts interior in a more modern dolls' house, wood sheet flooring is more suitable; finish with medium oak wood stain.

Fittings

The balusters and newel post are provided with this dolls' house, ready to stain and fit in place. Their design is equally suitable in a cottage or a more modern interior decorated in Arts & Crafts style. In this house they are stained medium oak but left unpolished, and the plain skirting boards and wooden cornice are stained to match.

The stairs

The stairs can be painted as stone or stained with oak wood stain. For a convincing worn look to stone stairs, it is worth going to extra trouble.

Method

1 After sanding, paint with a mixture of stone model enamel and off-white water-based paint.

2 Before the paint is completely dry, rub it off with white spirit.

3 Paint over with stone paint. When dry rub over with a damp cloth to leave a patchy effect.

Wallpaper or paint

Walls can be colour-washed with water-based paint: cream was the usual choice in an Arts & Crafts home. If you want a more rustic finish, as I did, use wallpaper with a rough texture to resemble plaster.

A plasterwork ceiling can be simulated with a textured wallpaper design intended for use on full-size ceilings. There are plenty of patterns to choose from and, provided you use one with a small-size repeat, it will look realistic. These papers are generally bright white, and it is worth painting the wallpaper with an off-white or cream water-based paint before pasting it in place.

12 The ceilings in the cottage are high enough to show off the realistic-looking 'plaster' ceiling.

13

14

15

13 A Windsor chair made in yew by a miniaturist who delights in fine chairs. A Windsor chair is not necessarily from Windsor, but the construction differs from other forms in that the back splats are fitted directly into the seat. The wooden seat is gently curved, making this type of chair reasonably comfortable.

14 A back view of the same Windsor hoopback elbow chair, with a nicely carved back splat and the much-admired feature of a bow-shaped stretcher.

15 A cottage-style piece popular with Arts & Crafts enthusiasts who had fled the town for a country life was a 'cricket' table. These were designed for use on uneven stone floors, as the three legs will always hold a table steady in places where four legs would rock. This miniature is made of yew; the glass teapot is hand-blown.

16 Useful rush-seated stools that continued in general use until the 1940s. Although the men would have turned the legs and made the frame, their wives would have woven the rush seats. The miniaturist reproduces the seat in 1:12 with bookbinder's linen thread, weaving the entire seat with one length, without joins.

16

Painted furniture

Most furniture was polished with beeswax to show off the beauty of the wood. Chests and buffets were sometimes painted in imitation of medieval style in order to appeal to those who, like the Pre-Raphaelite artists, had become enthralled by tales of knights and ladies and legends of court life.

17 Designed in Scotland, these are two distinctive pieces from my chair collection. The oak armchair is a copy of one by Charles Rennie Mackintosh (the original is in The Hill House, near Glasgow in Scotland) and the hooded chair is an Orkney chair, traditionally made from driftwood and rope, washed up by the tide on to local beaches.

18 This handpainted chest depicts a medieval scene, echoing the Arts & Crafts obsession with the simple life of an earlier age. The fine pewter jug is typical of handmade pewter sold in the London store Liberty, which specialized in Art Nouveau pewter.

The furniture

Plain furniture with the emphasis on quality is a hallmark of Arts & Crafts furniture. The craftsmen took such pride in their work that joints were often left exposed. Dovetails were a way of life!

Chairs were often adapted from traditional forms. The best-known chair introduced by Morris & Company was a more refined version of a prototype made by a craftsman in Sussex. I have sat on one and concluded that, like the famous chairs designed by Charles Rennie Mackintosh, they are pleasing to look at but not especially comfortable.

20

Kit furniture – make a revolving bookcase

The revolving bookcase in the bedroom of the cottage is a design that was first made in 1890, and more sophisticated versions are still made today. The kit I made up is based on one from the 1920s, towards the end of the Arts & Crafts period.

Woodturned miniatures

Turned miniatures enliven an Arts & Crafts interior. I am fascinated by woodturning – I have a large collection of full-size objects as well as the miniatures featured here and in other houses in this book (see pages 44 and 83). When watching turners at work, I am always amazed by their skill, and even more so when they are working in miniature.

However small the object, most turners still use a full-size lathe, running at a maximum speed of 2,300 revolutions per minute.

To see a miniaturist producing such a minute article, keeping hold of it without it flying away and disappearing, challenges the eyesight. As one turner mentioned to me: 'You do burn your fingers a bit, but you get used to it.'

Makers of dolls' house furniture sometimes like to turn small objects to use up their off-cuts, and there are often beautiful examples on show at miniatures fairs. I have also seen tiny goblets at crafts fairs, displayed with some pride by the makers of full-size bowls and plates. It is always worth keeping an eye open for such miniature treasures.

19 Kit parts to assemble a revolving bookcase. Although it may not look it, the kit is very straightforward to make up.

20 The completed bookcase has plenty of space for books – and it does revolve.

21 A collection of woodturned bowls and storage jars displayed on an oak table with a slatted lower shelf. The table was made from 400-year-old oak salvaged after a fire at Salisbury Cathedral.

22

22 An attractive design for a 20th-century occasional table; the clever construction of the stretchers, attached to the open end supports, is a homage to Arts & Crafts design. On top, more woodturnings include a pair of goblets, one in sycamore and one in ebony.

23 So tiny in 1:12 that they are made in bone, not wood, this pen with a silver nib and its companion piece, a rolling blotter, were made by a master turner who specializes in miniature work. The pen is kept in the desk drawer in the bedroom of my Georgian house (for fear of it rolling away), and needless to say, these are two of my most treasured miniatures.

23

Part two
European houses

Chapter 8
French farmhouse

In real life, the French style of living holds great appeal for many of us, especially for the British, who know that just across the English Channel, the narrow stretch of sea that divides Britain and France, there is better weather and a relaxed lifestyle in idyllic countryside, as well as distinctly different and very attractive building styles.

Drawn by this idea, many people do go to live in France, to find that the reality does not always match their imagination: restoring a dilapidated home can be very hard work, although ultimately rewarding.

When you build a French-style dolls' house from a kit, there are none of the problems with initial restoration. Assembly will be enjoyable, and

when completed, you will have a dolls' house with all the typically French features that you wanted. This house – 'St Remy' – is based on a *mas* (farmhouse), with shutters, wide double entrance doors and

2 The main parts of the kit are put together, and the staircase flights assembled. The interior of the house can be partly decorated before the staircase is painted and glued in place.

1 The typically French façade of the farmhouse, assembled from a kit. Vine leaves trail above the shutters and plants in tubs line the terrace.

3 The front is hinged on and the dormers fitted to the lift-off front portion of the roof.

dormer windows. Inside, there are four high-ceilinged rooms and a staircase that rises from the entrance to a loft that runs the whole width of the house. The kit was designed by a British dolls' house maker who has already taken the step of moving to live in France himself, so it is certainly authentic.

The assembly

This kit is of plywood, the choice of the traditionalist woodworker. Unlike some of the other kits featured in this book, these instructions consist of a list that describes all the parts, an exploded working drawing showing the complete assembly, plus a drawing of the façade, and an internal view with the position of the staircase already marked.

First, compare the list with the drawing, which is numbered 1 to 20 showing each stage of assembly. A dotted line indicates clearly where one part is fixed to another. You may need to look at all this several times to make sure that you understand each stage; if you are not used to working from a drawing it may at first appear baffling, but you will quickly find, as I did, that you are able to follow it easily.

Next, lay out all the parts, check them over and compare them with the working drawing. Once you have sorted this out, then you are ready to begin.

Taking your time, glue, pin and tape one section together and leave until the glue is set before you begin to assemble the next section.

TIP

When assembling a plywood kit, in addition to using wood glue, it is essential to pin the parts together with panel pins, which are easy to knock in. They will prevent any movement in the plywood. (See advice on kit assembly on page 162.)

The parts such as window frames and shutters are not finished to a ready-to-paint standard, which is perhaps something that is reflected in the very reasonable price of this kit. The finishing is something that you can easily do yourself. Careful sanding will produce a smooth surface ready to decorate and help you to achieve a professional finish.

4 Trying for size. The shutters are temporarily attached with adhesive putty to judge the effect before removing them for sanding and painting.

5 The window frames are not a tight fit in the apertures. Fill any gaps with interior filler and, when dry, sand smooth before undercoating and painting. The glazing bars will also need to be sanded thoroughly: an emery board (as used for nail care) is effective and is easier to use than sandpaper between narrow spaces.

6 7 Two colours that are often chosen for shutters: the bright blue will look good against a pink façade, while the rust is more often used on an off-white exterior.

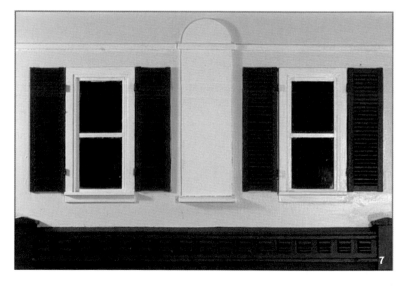

8 The doorknocker, like the ring handle, is in a burnished iron finish and was chosen to look more French than English.

This house is also available ready-made, but one of the advantages of assembling it from a kit is that you can paint the shutters before fixing them in place. Painting around fixed shutters involves the use of masking tape while the paint on the façade dries, and then the same process in reverse to avoid getting paint on the completed façade.

The exterior decoration

There are plenty of colour schemes that will look realistic on a French *mas* – off-white, stone, pale yellow or apricot are all suitable. Paintwork is usually white; shutters in any shade of blue, or sometimes a deep russet.

On my house I used a pale creamy-yellow for the façade, with pale blue for the shutters, to give a sun-bleached appearance. Off-white paintwork completes the look.

The roof is painted with two coats of mid-grey model enamel. If preferred you can add slates (see page 29). Or, if you imagine your house to be situated in Alsace or Languedoc-Roussillon then shingles, painted grey to simulate shaped tiles, will be appropriate.

You can provide authentic door furniture for the inside of the double entrance doors too. Most French houses in remote areas are heavily fortified, with bolts that are always used at night, and this will make a realistic addition.

9 These bolts are working models.

10 The inside front is papered with a regular wallpaper that is wide enough to cover it without a join. The colour was chosen to match the exterior. The windows are glazed with acetate and inner frames made from plain stripwood are painted to match the doors before gluing in place.

11 The principal rooms are decorated and furnished.

The inside of the opening front is wallpapered in a colour to match the exterior. This is a regular wallpaper sample, given extra interest with a few widely spaced gold motifs. It is always worth adding inside window frames, so that acetate glazing can be sandwiched between outer and inner frames. The *oeil-de-boeuf* window is there for ventilation, and so it is never glazed.

The interior

Many French farmhouses began life as manorial dwellings; at first prosperous, they often became run-down during and after the Napoleonic wars. Some even remained neglected until recently, when so many are being restored by the new wave of British residents.

This gives a variety of options for the dolls' house interior decorator; the rooms can be made to look 'original' and faded, or show the newly decorated but more casual look of today's holiday home. My aim was to achieve a comfortable, lived-in look but with traces of former grandeur, as the house might have appeared during the late 19th century.

The floors

Tiled floors are the most suitable for the rooms on the entrance floor of a French house like this one, and can be provided economically by using dolls' house tile paper, regular vinyl wallpaper, or plasticized sheet. All are easy to cut and glue in place and I found a variety of colours and patterns to choose from.

In the upstairs rooms, planked floors, cut from dolls' house wood sheet are stained walnut, the most commonly used wood for this purpose in France. The loft is partly divided into two by the top of the stairs, making it easy to have neat joins at this point. I found that running the central section of planking in the opposite direction gave the best effect here.

12 The farmer's gun and a storm lantern in the hall are both ready for use. The tiled floor is simulated in vinyl wallpaper, while the stone seat reinforces the countryside feeling. The stairs are scrubbed clean but show the passage of many feet over the years: to achieve this effect, sand the centre part of each tread a little before painting. Make the dips uneven, so that some treads will appear more worn than others.

13 A join in flooring is necessary in such a long room but the balusters at the top of the wide staircase provide a useful opportunity to make a neat join that looks intentional.

14 This is a working farmhouse kitchen, with meals in preparation for a hungry family. The striking floor tiling is merely black and white dolls' house floor paper. It may not last as long as hard flooring, but will be easy to replace when necessary.

Walls and ceilings

The simplest and most suitable treatment for the ceilings is to paint with off-white, water-based paint. In a farmhouse some of the walls might be roughly plastered. The easiest way to achieve this effect is to use wallpaper with some texture and paint it in the colour you want. I did this in the hall, the kitchen and the loft, while the main rooms are wallpapered.

15 Farm produce will be used to provide delicious meals.

The kitchen

The kitchen is one of the most important rooms in a French farmhouse. A continental stove and an armoire create an authentic French look. The tile paper flooring looks striking and contrasts well with the deep pink walls, which are warm and welcoming.

The dining room

On the other side of the hall, the dining room is tiled in a rich red and cream that reminded me of the floors in Monet's home, which I have visited on holiday. I trimmed away the Victorian-style border, which was part of this plasticized sheet. A meal is in progress, with plenty of vin rouge to complement a substantial meal.

The bedroom

The bedroom has been decorated and furnished to look elegant and feminine and I imagine that the distinctively French-style furniture (from an inexpensive mail order range) might have been in the house before it became a farmhouse.

16 The dining room is always of first importance in a French house. Solid furniture, with benches rather than chairs, will provide enough space for any latecomers.

17 The impressive fireplace has space for a log fire to provide plenty of warmth on cold winter days.

I repainted all these pieces in a soft, pale green, which creates a lighter effect than the original mahogany stain.

The empire-style bed

Similar styles of bed were used during the period when Napoleon was Emperor of France, and they were often decorated with gilded mouldings.

After painting with satin-finish paint, I added some gilt flower-shaped buttons and drapes made from ribbon. Decorative 'gold' buttons that look like metal are

in fact more often made from plastic, and it is easy to cut off the shank with wire cutters or pliers to give a flatter back.

Method

1 Cut off the shank with wire cutters or pliers.

2 Mark and drill a hole at each corner of the bed, making it large enough to take the truncated shank, and glue the button in place.

3 Arrange ribbon drapes and attach to the wall. Add a gilt moulding at the top to complete the effect.

18 The bedroom has an air of comfort, with a carpet on the wooden floor and a small fireplace, which I painted in a light stone shade.

The loft

A large loft like this one, with dormer windows to let in plenty of light, can be used for many different purposes, depending on your ideas for the rest of the house. It can become a children's playroom, or in a house updated for modern use, a holiday apartment.

In this house, one end of the loft is a simple bedroom for a visitor or a servant. The other end is sparsely furnished with a painted double seat.

21 A plain, roughly finished table is suitable for a farmhouse kitchen. The country pottery, made in France, includes a bowl filled with 'sugar' and complete with a spoon.

22 This chest of drawers was made by a professional miniaturist and demonstrates how a plain piece can become decorative.

19 A plain, low bed, a rather battered double seat and a painted chest of drawers furnish the bedroom in the loft. The woven mat on the floor is a small table mat.

20 The small stove in the loft is an inexpensive model that might, perhaps, provide a modicum of heat. Two large green glass flagons for wine and a wooden tub to store apples also find a place here.

23

24

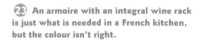 **An armoire with an integral wine rack is just what is needed in a French kitchen, but the colour isn't right.**

24 The repainted armoire displays copper pans, hand-blown glass wine bottles in jewel colours, and a set of jugs, all made in France, while in front there are more pottery flagons and vessels.

Repaint ready-made furniture

The armoire in the farmhouse kitchen was finished as mahogany, and was perfectly acceptable but inappropriate in its French setting. I sanded it carefully, then painted it with green model enamel to match the table bases in the same room.

Although it was easy to paint around the brass knobs on the drawers, I prised off the fancy handles on the two lower drawers and re-glued them in place after the paint was dry.

Make a blanket box from a kit

A wooden blanket box would be useful for storage in a French farmhouse, and might find a place in the loft.

25 The parts to make up a blanket box.

26 The completed blanket box is nicely detailed, with rounded feet and a panelled front. It is shown here unpolished but can be finished by rubbing over with fine grade wire wool and then with a wax polish.

There is also some wine-making equipment, but enough space for further additions at a future date.

The furniture

You may need to adapt or repaint ready-made furniture to give it a distinctively French appearance. Here are a few ideas.

Paint whitewood furniture

A plain chest of drawers can be painted and decorated to suit a French room. First sand it until smooth, then paint with satin-finish paint – a mid-green is always a useful colour. Use bought transfers to add sprays of flowers (a technique known as decoupage); designs in 1:12 scale are widely available.

25

26

Chapter 9
French manor house

This French-style dolls' house was bought fully assembled and ready to decorate. The exterior has features in common with the farmhouse made from a kit, but with some architectural additions that are more appropriate for its use as a manor house. It offers opportunities to try out a grander style.

The manor house has a parapet, a pediment, a pilastered front and two sets of French doors, as well as shutters that can be opened and closed. These give it a more formal appearance than the simple farmhouse, so I chose to decorate and furnish the interior accordingly.

This particular model is no longer available, but serves as an example: the decorative schemes can be used in any house, ready-built or made from a kit, where you fancy a little grandeur and a distinctive French

look. For this, there is no shortage of suitable dolls' houses from a number of makers.

The exterior decoration

Perhaps the best-known colour scheme for a French country house, familiar to us from countless pictures in travel brochures, books and on postcards, is the deep pink façade with turquoise-green shutters and white paintwork that Monet chose for his home at Giverny, in Normandy, France. When first painted the colours are vivid, but gradually fade to a softer hue, so you will need to decide which of these you prefer for your dolls' house.

① **Pretty as a picture! White paintwork emphasizes the architectural details on the manor house.**

② **The house before decoration. The smooth finish of this professionally made house did not need sanding, so decoration could begin immediately.**

3 Bright colour contrasts look good in a sunny climate, and this colour scheme is popular in France.

The spacious loft is typical of French country houses, and runs the whole length of the roof space. The front part of the roof lifts off for access, while the back remains fixed, and the *oeil-de-boeuf* window in the centre of the pediment allows a bird's-eye view of this top storey.

To establish the manorial ambience instantly, the entrance hall is given a formal appearance with a silk-covered seat for the convenience of visitors. The stone table holds a French-style basket filled with roses, and there is a hydrangea in a Provençal pot placed just inside the front door.

I like the gently faded look, so my manor house is painted in a soft apricot, with the pale blue shutters that are always my first choice. White, or a deeper mid-blue, are good alternatives. Shutters that I can be opened and closed must, of course, be painted on both sides.

4 Paint shades were kept to a minimum for a coordinated look, but wallpapers and flooring are varied in design and colour.

To avoid accidental closure while the paint dries on each side, prop them open with a wooden cocktail stick, which will stay firmly in place in a groove of the shutter.

Interior arrangements

There are four main rooms, an entrance hall and a landing above the staircase that is wide enough to be used as an extra room.

5 The entrance hall looks cool and shady, a refuge from the heat outside.

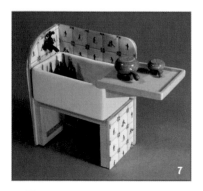

6 Stoneware vessels and baskets are used for storage in the kitchen, while a capacious armoire will hold pottery and pans.

The kitchen

Food is of paramount importance in France, so let's begin our tour of the rooms with the kitchen. A Continental stove looks its best against a panel of plasticized tile sheet simulating French ceramic tiles. The stove is raised up on a piece of wood, ½in (12mm) thick, which is also covered with the same tile sheet.

7 Wine bottles have been rinsed in the sink and casserole dishes left to dry on the draining board, giving the kitchen a well-used look.

8 Guests will gather for a glass of wine before sitting down to lunch in this charming room.

9 A flower painting over the staircase is the finishing touch to a well-used space.

This kitchen has a capacious armoire to contain clutter, and also a sink. The plain whitewood base and splashback have also been given a French look with the tile sheet.

The salon

In Britain, and in other countries, the separate dining room is fast disappearing, as eating in the kitchen is now acceptable even when guests are present. In France, however, a formal dining room is still considered essential, although if space is short it may be sited at one end of a reception room. For this reason I decided to combine the dolls' house dining room and salon.

The wallpaper, with a tiny printed design of fleur-de-lis, is a full-sized wallpaper that seemed eminently suitable for this dolls' house.

The floor, made from plasticized sheet, mimics a Provençal tile pattern. A classical marble bust in a corner makes it clear that this is a salon or reception room.

There is enough space on the landing for an escritoire and a chair, so that it can be used as a writing room. The attractive floor, with the appearance of old tiles, is thin card from a stationer's. One traditional use for an armoire is for storing linen and I found this very enjoyable to arrange.

10 As well as blankets, a pillow and fine linen sheets, the neatly folded quilts are of *toile de Jouy* fabrics that are much treasured in Provence. Each is tied with a narrow ribbon and finished with a bow to make them look even more special.

The bedrooms

A French manor house bedroom can be very elegant, and *toile de Jouy* was often chosen as a wall covering. The distinctive deep pink on white was a popular colour choice, and designs are available as 1:12 wallpaper as well as in two fabrics, one cotton and one fine silk. In the 18th and early 19th centuries, the fabric was tacked onto wooden battens that were fixed to the walls, but for a dolls' house using wallpaper makes decorating simpler.

To add to the luxurious appearance of this bedroom, I improvised a carpet by using a piece of papyrus (from stockists of art papers). When laid on the floor, it has the appearance of a silk carpet.

It is quite fragile, so is best glued on to thin card before fixing it with double-sided adhesive tape along each edge of the card. A 1:12 carpet would also be suitable; if you enjoy needlework you could work a petit-point carpet from a kit or chart.

The mahogany furniture with cane insets suits this room perfectly. French bedrooms often feature elaborately carved furniture, which to British eyes can seem rather old-fashioned, but here is just right. As an alternative, paint whitewood furniture with pale grey matt paint.

I chose a flower-sprigged wallpaper for the second bedroom, which is arranged as though for the daughter

11 I do not include dolls in my dolls' houses very often, but the French-made doll in the bedroom is an exception, as I have had her for many years. Finally she has a room to suit her!

12 A *toile de Jouy* cotton quilt is laid over the bed and a square, French-style pillow is covered in silk toile to match the wallpaper.

13 I used a plain wooden bed in this bedroom, but an old-fashioned metal bed with brass knobs might be even more appropriate.

of the house. Older country houses are notoriously short of bathrooms; I have added a 'marble'-topped washstand from an inexpensive range of ready-made furniture and a blue-and-white china toilet set, both of which would certainly have been in use until recently.

The loft

I decided on an unstained wooden floor for this loft. A division is provided by a thin strip of plain moulding, and a screen can be arranged to make it into two separate rooms. One end of the loft is used to store Christmas decorations and toys. The other end provides a quiet place to sit and read. It might be a retreat for an artist, a place to do school homework, or a study for an author.

14 The loft has plenty of room for a selection of furniture and other objects and it is easy to change the contents without redecoration.

15 Another, more rustic version of a *toile de Jouy* dolls' house wallpaper depicts scenes of rural life. It is available in blue, grey, green or red on a white background.

Decorating the manor house

I used wallpaper in all the rooms for a luxurious effect. For the bedrooms I chose 1:12 designs, but in the hall I used a thicker art paper to resemble stone and in the kitchen a textured wallpaper to look like plaster.

The ceilings are all painted off-white, but in some of the rooms I added beams. Most French country houses have beamed ceilings but the beams are rather different from those in an English house.

To make them, cut and distress wooden dowel (see page 18). The beams should be arranged in a grid pattern rather than widely spaced. For an average-size dolls' house room, try three main beams across, with smaller beams in between, at approximately 2in (50mm) intervals.

Other fittings

When you decorate a dolls' house in a style from a country you may not be familiar with, it is essential to get the small details correct.

If you include skirting boards, try to find a wood moulding about ¾in (19mm) high, as standard Georgian-style dolls' house skirtings will be inappropriate. A straight moulding with a groove in it, or one with a rounded edge, will look just a little different from one that features in an English or American house.

Paint skirtings and ceiling beams a matt greyish-white, to look like untreated, aged wood. If you include ceiling beams then you will not be able to add cornices – it can be tricky to hang wallpaper accurately from the top of a wall when there is no cornice to cover the join between wall and ceiling. When you paint the ceiling, extend the paint about ½in (12mm) down on to the wall, so that if after wallpapering there is a minuscule gap, it will be not be noticeable.

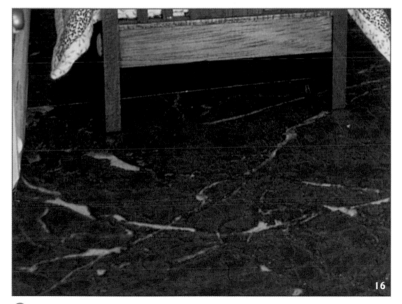

at a corner of the card base, lay the sheet in place a little at a time. Note that this material adheres instantly when the backing is peeled off and is difficult to remove once stuck down.

3 Gently peel off the backing and smooth the sheet in place. This does take some care, but fortunately this material is inexpensive so if your first attempt goes wrong, you can start again!

4 Finally attach the complete floor in place using double-sided adhesive tape.

16 Dark-coloured marble makes an attractive background for the bedroom furniture.

Flooring

Floors of plasticized tile sheet predominate but there are other possibilities. Flagstones, brick or marble can be used in a manor house, while in bedrooms there may be carpet rather than bare boards. To make a contrast with the tiled floors in adjacent rooms, the flooring in the entrance hall of this house is textured brick sheet in a herringbone pattern. This can be cut with scissors and glued in place with PVA adhesive.

Fit a marble floor

The second bedroom has a marble floor. To simulate marble, use self-adhesive plasticized sheet from the hardware store. It is sold from 18in (460mm) wide rolls and can be bought by the yard or metre. Choose the marbled design carefully and it will look extremely realistic.

Method

1 Make a thin card pattern the size of the floor and use it as a guide to cut the self-adhesive plastic sheet.

2 To avoid wrinkles forming while fitting, begin by gently peeling off one corner of the backing. Starting

The furniture

The ready-made French-style furniture in the manor house all came from inexpensive ranges that are available through dolls' house shops and by mail order. The green-painted Provençal-style suite is absolutely authentic, and this furniture is still much used in French country houses.

17 A marble-topped Louis XVI low table made by a master craftsman. The handcarved base was cast in pewter, hand-finished and then gilded with 22 carat gold.

18 A gilt torchère of about 1700; it would have been used as a candle stand or to hold a silver or china jar.

19 A Louis XV console table, designed to rest against a wall. The top is of Italian marble. Above it, a mirror in a gilded frame looks equally magnificent.

20 A mirror with a frame made from a picture of an antique French mirror cut from a glossy magazine.

18

19

Method

1 Cut a piece of fake mirror glass a little larger than the aperture for the mirror, and glue it onto a backing of thin card.

2 Cut card backing the same size as the paper frame and draw the outline of the glass centrally on it.

3 Glue the 'glass' to the backing, then glue the pictured frame on top. This method can be used to provide a mirror of the correct period style for any dolls' house room.

If you plan a manor house full of antique furniture rather than the simpler pieces I have chosen, you may prefer to use gilded furniture.

Make a mirror frame

To make a mirror like the one over the fireplace in the French bedroom, you will need to find a magazine picture of a real French antique mirror. Any suitable picture can be reduce-photocopied in colour and the space for the glass cut out.

20

21 An occasional table with a removable tray is a useful piece. Add gold detail with a fine brush or use a gold fineline pen.

Painted furniture

Painted furniture will always find a place in a French manor. I used an exceptionally pretty occasional table with matching removable tray, painted in mid-green with gold trim, that was professionally made. You might like to try painting a whitewood piece in a similar manner and add a transfer flower spray.

A table to make from a kit

Furniture made from kits can also be painted. A low table with rococo legs made from a whitewood kit is very suitable. One of these might go in a hall, or a pair could be placed in alcoves on either side of a fireplace or on opposite sides of a room, to provide the symmetrical look that the French love in their interiors.

22 This low table is very easy to assemble from a whitewood kit.

23 The completed table, painted with a matt finish paint in a pale greeny-grey. The paint has been rubbed down in places to give a look of age.

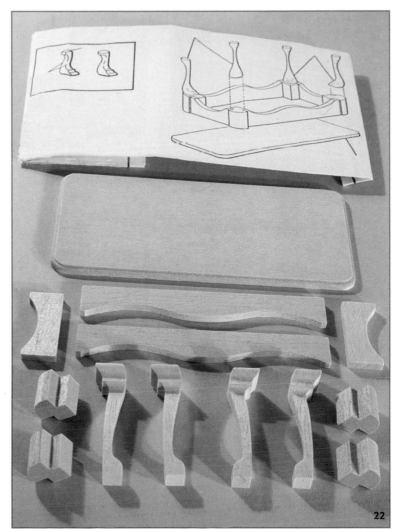

Chapter 10
Dutch canal-side house

This unusual dolls' house is a scaled-down replica of a 17th-century canal-side house in Amsterdam. Even if you have not visited the Netherlands, you are probably familiar with these houses from pictures in books or magazines: the distinctive façades immediately identify them as Dutch.

The sight of a terrace of these houses, with curving gable-ends, alongside a canal is breathtaking. After dark, when the lights inside are lit and reflections shine in the water, the effect is magical.

This dolls' house was designed by an English maker, whose imagination was caught on a trip to the Netherlands. Many photographs and visits later, the prototype was completed. The house kit is simple enough for beginners to tackle.

❶ The Dutch house is 36⅝in high, 17⅞in wide and 16⅛in deep (950 x 455 x 410mm). The maker deliberately designed it to be slightly wider than the tall, narrow houses of Amsterdam, to allow more space for the hobbyist to furnish the rooms.

❷ Unpacking and laying out the parts gives a good indication of how the house will be assembled. Although not fixed, the windows are in place on the façade initially, which helps to show how it will look when completed.

The kit assembly

This kit is made from MDF (medium density fibreboard), which does not warp or twist and takes a paint finish well. The only snag is its weight – I could manage this one on my own, but would have needed help with a larger model. There are just nine pieces to assemble to make the basic structure. The smaller parts are architectural mouldings, doors, windows and a ready-assembled staircase. So no one need be daunted by what, initially, seems to be a large number of parts. The picture on the outside of the pack is also reassuring, showing the completed dolls' house.

The instructions

The instructions are very easy to follow. The maker does not waste time on details that would be obvious from the picture, or put in any unnecessary diagrams, but gets straight down to basics – a simple, numbered list of points and five clear drawings showing exactly how to fit the main parts together. And the beauty of this house, with its three floors and an attic, is that the main parts are so easy to slide into the pre-cut grooves.

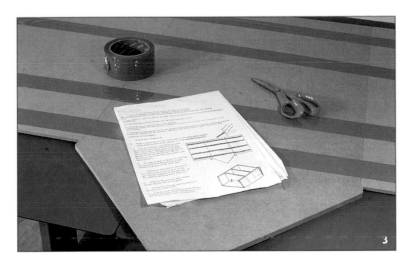

3 The walls are laid flat, taped together with parcel tape on the plain side, then turned over so that the tape is underneath and the grooves on top, ready for gluing.

4 Glue the floors into the grooves at the back, then lift the side walls up, one at a time, and glue the floors into the side grooves. This is where some help from a friend will be useful, to make sure that everything is pushed together firmly before fixing more parcel tape until the glue has set.

The grooves are exactly the right size. No nails or screws are necessary, just wood glue, and parcel tape to hold the parts together while the glue sets. The method is clearly shown in the drawings.

When the basic shell is assembled, it is time to hinge on the front, a task viewed with apprehension by miniaturists who may not have tackled a kit assembly before. This maker has chosen cranked hinges

for attaching the front and these must be far and away the best type of hinge for this purpose. When compared with the more usual butt hinges, the ease with which you can accurately screw on a cranked hinge cannot be over-emphasized. They also present a neat appearance inside the dolls' house.

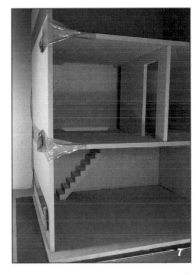

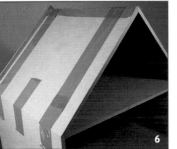

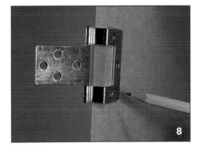

5 The main structure is now assembled, ready for the roof to be added.

6 The two sections of roof are taped together before they are glued in place.

7 The staircase shown in position under the pre-cut stairwell. The room dividers can be placed where you choose to make two rooms on each floor, or omitted if you want one really large room.

8 The cranked hinges supplied with this kit are very easy for the hobbyist to fit.

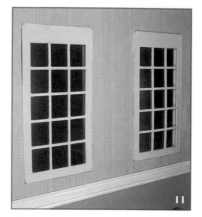

⑨ Blue-grey window frames make a good contrast against the off-white architectural mouldings on the façade.

⑩ The right-hand inner window frame and glazing have been fitted; the other remains to be glued in place.

⑪ Both these windows are now in place.

Completing the façade

The final stage of the kit assembly is to add all the decorative mouldings to the façade. But before you do this it is sensible to paint them, as you will want to use different colours for the window frames and the trim that butts against them.

All the mouldings fit neatly into clearly marked places that are slightly indented, and can be taped in position with masking tape to ensure that they do not shift while the glue sets. The long vertical strips in particular need to be taped firmly in place so that they lie flat at both ends and do not spring up. I found it easiest to lay the house flat on its back and glue the mouldings in place while it was horizontal, therefore preventing any movement through gravity.

The windows, complete with glazing bars, are of styrene, which can be painted if a colour is preferred to white. The inside front should be painted or papered first, and acetate

glazing cut and glued in place before adding the windows. A shallow indentation makes it easy to do this.

The last step before completing the decorations is to fit the double entrance doors on to the façade. The doors are hung above a shallow step, so there is enough space to add flooring inside the room without fear of the doors catching when opened.

The hinges are attached with round-headed brass screws, which present an attractive appearance. To look neat they are necessarily small, which requires patience, but the instructions for fitting are clear so that even a beginner should have no difficulty. Just ensure that you have the right size of screwdriver to hand!

⑫ There is a good view of the interior through the double entrance doors and arcaded front windows.

make a template from stiff paper and check the fit carefully before cutting the brick sheet.

The brickwork can be left as supplied, or made to look weathered and aged by painting. Simulate grime by using watered-down black and grey acrylic paint in places where this would have happened naturally – look at a real brick house anywhere, not necessarily in the Netherlands, to see where this occurs. Try out your painting technique on a spare piece of brick sheet first. As well as using a brush, a finger can be useful to smudge the painted area so that it looks natural.

13 Brick cladding, carefully aged with paint to give the appearance of 200 years of weathering, on the gable end.

Finish the façade with brick

The 17th-century houses in Amsterdam are renowned for the beauty of their brickwork, but like English Tudor houses, the brick may be an addition to a house that was originally of timber. The houses in this waterlogged city, where the sea is kept at bay by dykes, are all built on wooden piles.

Sheets of textured brick cladding are ideal to use on a Dutch house. To fit brick cladding in between the mouldings or on the gable end,

14 These rooms have been arranged by a hobbyist with a talent for creating a lived-in look. To make an extra-large living room, she omitted the staircase, and filled the gap before adding flooring. The rooms at this stage are partly furnished while decisions are made. It is always a good idea to try out different ideas before you finalize any scheme.

15

15 This beautiful floor was made from more than 250 tiles. The tiles were cut and fitted individually before being painted and distressed.

The gable end

The gable ends of these houses were sometimes heavily ornamented to emphasize the status of the owner. Wealthy merchants competed to see whose house would be the most elaborate – such display was definitely a form of 17th-century one-upmanship. The example shown is restrained, with just two plaster mouldings and a brass motif at the top. I think this not-too-fancy look suits a dolls' house. You could also add a date, or any trim that looks like stone.

A traditional Dutch interior

The interiors of old Dutch houses are familiar to us through paintings, and more recently they have been accurately depicted on film – such as *The Girl With The Pearl Earring*, adapted from Tracy Chevalier's novel which is based on Vermeer's famous painting.

The decorations

To reproduce this gently aged look, walls and ceilings can be colour-washed in cream, which can be smoothly painted or roughened to give the appearance of plaster. (See the French farmhouse on page 108.)

Floors are tiled in chequerboard black and white, or coloured in red-brown and ochre, green and grey. Plasticized tile sheet does not give quite the right impression here, so it would be worthwhile to make and fit individual tiles.

To make a tiled floor

Tiles can be square or hexagonal. Packets of card templates can be bought from craft shops, but these will wear quickly if you are cutting a large number of tiles. You will need to change the template often to avoid your tiles gradually becoming smaller. Metal templates (used for patchwork) from needlework stockists will wear better.

Method

1 Cut a sheet of thin card to fit the floor of the room.

2 Plan out your design on the card, with the aid of a template, so that any part-cut tiles necessary to fit the floor will be at the back and evenly spaced against each side wall.

3 Cut the tiles from two different colours of card. There will be a huge range of colours in your local craft shop but note that art mounting

board is too thick for this purpose, as it will be too difficult to cut small tiles with safety.

4 Alternatively use white card and paint the required number of tiles in each of two colours.

5 Glue the tiles onto the card base with PVA adhesive. It is not essential to grout them, although if you want to give this appearance it can be simulated by carefully painting in between the tiles with grey paint, using a fine brush. This is a very time-consuming process and I would recommend omitting grout!

TIP

As a quick alternative to making a tiled floor from individual tiles, look out for card printed with a pattern of old tiles. The brown, russet and black floor in the French manor house on page 115 is card from a craft shop.

16 A quick solution: card printed to look like old tiles can be used to make a floor.

16

17 An impressive fireplace with a fine display of pottery on the mantel and cupboards on either side filled with more pots create the balanced look so admired by the Dutch. The dark oak table shows off a set piece of fruit, flowers and pewter – an idea taken from Dutch paintings of the era.

Planked floors, stained dark, can be added to the upstairs rooms, although tiled floors are not uncommon there too. With a tiled floor, you do not necessarily need to fit skirting boards. One interesting idea shown in 17th-century Dutch paintings is a tile skirting made from blue and white ceramic tiles. For a really luxurious effect, 1:12 Delft tiles could be used.

18 The bedroom also serves as a nursery for a small child. This arrangement, with the partition wall placed towards the back of the room, gives a view through as though to a smaller room beyond, an effect often seen in Dutch paintings. A collection of miniature samplers shows up well on the roughly plastered walls.

19

The gable-end allows space for a good-sized attic. This has many possible uses – maybe for storage, for old furniture, or for framed paintings or canvases stacked against the walls.

19 The lacquer furniture in the attic seems too good to have been relegated, but perhaps is merely awaiting relocation to another room. Japanese and Chinese lacquer was imported by the Dutch East India Company during the 17th century and displayed in the homes of wealthy merchants.

20 A well-used nursery contains a collection of toys miniaturized from early examples.

20

The furniture

Here are some pieces of ready-made furniture that will reinforce an antique effect. Although dark wood predominated, the interiors would not have seemed dark as the huge windows let in plenty of light.

Richness and colour was added by draping carpets over tables or coffers and hanging patterned curtains; chairs were often upholstered in blue or red leather.

Wealthy merchants enjoyed displaying their possessions; you might like to include blue-and-white Delftware and pewter. Dutch 'Old Master' paintings in dark wooden frames will look their best against plain walls.

22

21

21 A corner cupboard on a matching table base, open to show the pewter jugs inside. The carving on the panelled front is typical of Dutch furniture of the period.

22 The corner table shown without its matching cupboard, which can be mounted on a wall if preferred. On top, a glazed earthenware lidded dish with slip decoration.

23 A high chair for a child can be used in the nursery or at meal times.

24 A heavily carved settle that could be used in almost any room.

23

24

25 26 An alternative scheme for the upper two floors. The attic now provides storage for furniture waiting to be used in another dolls' house, while on the floor below a bedroom, with a cradle for a new baby, is in course of arrangement.

Painted furniture

Painted furniture is also much used in the Netherlands to this day. Why not paint some whitewood furniture yourself? Try to find something with pretty detail, rather than a plain piece. The following method will ensure a really good finish.

Method

1 Sand the piece over lightly with fine grade sandpaper, even if it seems smooth already.

2 Acrylic paint works well on whitewood furniture. Choose a soft shade that will look good against stained or polished furniture in the same room.

3 To give it an aged look, distress the piece by rubbing back the paint when dry to leave small areas of bare wood in places where wear would occur naturally, such as at corners or on the lower part of legs or on rails.

27 A whitewood side table with a drawer and curving front detail has been painted in a soft grey and distressed slightly to show wear.

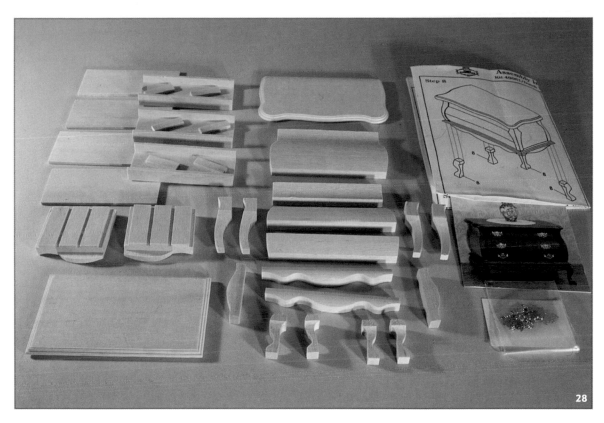

28

29

A kit to make an authentic Dutch commode

Here is a kit to make a curvaceous Dutch bombe commode. With three drawers to assemble and fit, curving corner posts and shaped trim, this is more complicated than the kits shown earlier, but provided you take your time and follow the instructions exactly you will end up with a fine commode for your Dutch house.

28 There are a lot of parts to make up in this kit. Apart from the usual sanding before assembly, the ends of the legs must be sanded down to produce gently curving, rounded feet.

29 The completed commode can be stained but looks even better painted and distressed.

Chapter 11
Dutch museum

I spend much of my leisure time in museums, especially those that specialize in the decorative arts. Seeing furniture and paintings displayed in room settings as they would have been during different periods is immensely useful to a dolls' house decorator, providing a three-dimensional view to supplement pictures in books on architecture, decoration and furniture.

This house as a museum is an example of a conventional dolls' house put to a dramatically different new use, inspired by seeing Wellington's own homes.

But as well as domestic interiors, I have another, completely different interest: in the events that took place in the late 18th and early 19th centuries during the Napoleonic wars. Studying the broad sweep of military campaigns provides a refreshing contrast from the minutia of domestic interiors.

I have been to Waterloo and walked the battlefield and have seen Napoleon's tomb in Paris. I have visited the country home of the

great Duke of Wellington, Stratfield Saye House, as well as his London home, known as No. 1 London, which is now a fascinating museum.

As well as military trophies, these two great houses naturally include splendid furniture, paintings and sculpture acquired by the Duke during his long career, providing

① The colours of this façade are based on paintings showing houses and street scenes by Jan Vermeer and Pieter de Hooch, using a palette of off-whites, soft greenish-greys and blue-greys, and with a bold accent of red.

③ Wellington sizes up the enemy. On the battlefield, he always wore a plain, dark blue coat.

② Shutters are one of the features of canal-side houses, whose function was as a home for a merchant combined with warehouse storage for his business. These shutters, of unequal size, can be closed against rain while allowing some light into the attic room from one side.

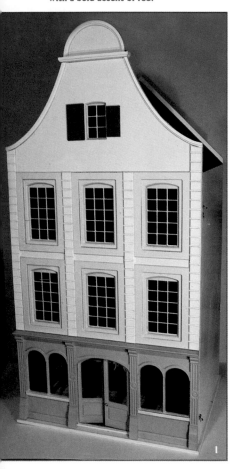

4 Wellington is a resplendent figure in full-dress uniform, which would be worn for ceremonial occasions.

a reminder of a home life lived in a grand manner after his retirement from military duties.

This project is a second scheme for the Dutch dolls' house made from the same kit as the previous project. In this version, I have arranged it as a museum to hold my collection of military models. The Dutch connection seemed appropriate, as the Dutch fought alongside the British to defeat Napoleon.

The exterior decoration

Houses in Amsterdam dating from the 17th century are faced with brick, but in other Dutch cities some canal-side houses have stucco fronts. A painted façade, imitating stucco, is quicker and easier to achieve than covering the house with cladding, but I decided to use paint mainly because of my intended use for this dolls' house. The contents would provide enough colour and excitement, so as a contrast, I wanted to keep the façade calm and neutral.

5 The colonnade effect on the entrance floor is appropriate for a house used as a museum. I left these windows unglazed, so that a *trompe l'oeil* effect at the back is reinforced when you look in.

The interior

Without the room dividers put in position, the spacious rooms, each measuring 8⅛in high, 18⅛in wide and 15¼in deep (205 x 460 x 385mm) provide large display areas for a collection, whether of military models or some other specialization.

I decided not to include the staircase, which would have hidden part of my chosen *trompe l'oeil* wallpaper on the entrance floor, and to leave even more space for models on the floors above.

Depending on your use for the house, you might prefer to have a staircase or, as here, simply to imagine its existence, along with other rooms behind.

6 The interior is decorated and ready to arrange the model collection. I have always had a weakness for miniature chairs, perhaps one of the greatest tests of skill for any maker. Those in the corners of the rooms are placed as though for use by museum attendants.

If you have decided against putting in a staircase, then before you do anything else to the interior you will need to measure the stairwell space and cut and glue in MDF pieces to fill the gap on each floor. You can cut these to size from the unwanted pieces designed to fit in front of the stairs, as this material will be of the right thickness.

7 The uniformed figures show up well against the richly coloured walls. As well as the seated and standing figures, there is some action going on in each room; the smaller models are from ready-made boxed sets.

Arranging the dolls' house as a museum provides an opportunity to try out decorations in a different style from a home, and still introduce period wallpaper. I was able to include a few pieces of 1:12 furniture to supplement the military models that are in a variety of scales, as they might be in a real museum.

The entrance floor

The magnificent library setting was achieved by using a dolls' house wallpaper that simulates shelves full of books. This paper is available in three versions: the one with shelves of books and a marble dado below; a variation with portrait medallions among the books; and one that I chose for the back wall, to give a *trompe l'oeil* effect of a corridor leading through other rooms beyond.

8 9 The library is full of interest and provides a splendid introduction to the museum collection.

⑩ Nelson's flagship is reproduced in the smallest scale possible while still including so much detail.

⑪ Admiral Lord Nelson is an easily recognizable figure.

⑫ This small tableau of a naval commander and a marine, about to fire on the enemy, is one of a number of recent models produced after film successes dealing with military and naval exploits. If you look carefully, you will see that this figure is based on the actor Russell Crowe.

Trompe l'oeil wallpapers are available depicting plainly panelled rooms, as well as some with panels complete with painted decoration in a variety of styles, including chinoiserie.

The entrance hall floor is tiled in black-and-white plasticized sheet flooring, which has been carefully and invisibly joined to cover the large space. Joining the pieces is easy when the pattern is a geometric design: simply use the printed lines as a guide.

A naval hero

The British Navy played a large part in the downfall of Napoleon by preventing his ships from playing a major part in his strategies after his defeat at Trafalgar. The British Navy is represented in the library, with portraits of Admiral Lord Nelson. A matching pair of inexpensive, glass-topped display cabinets show off souvenirs: in one, there is a miniature book on the Battle of Trafalgar; in the other, a brass expanding telescope. On top of this second table, brilliantly executed in 1:144 scale, a model of Nelson's flagship, *The Victory*, takes pride of place.

My collection continued to grow and a figure of Nelson and a tableau of a ship's commander with a marine are now also on show in the library.

The upper rooms

Wallpapers for the upper rooms are in deep, military-looking colours, chosen to make a suitable background for the splendid uniforms. The floors are all of walnut, left unpolished, and the ceilings are papered with embossed paper in imitation of plaster relief.

13 Red and gold make a brilliant background for Wellington and his men. The painting on the back wall is of Sergeant Masterman capturing the first eagle to be taken in the Peninsular War. An Irishman, he is reported to have exclaimed: 'Bejabbers, boys, I have their cuckoo.'

14 An impressive console table with a real marble top. The eagle base was handcarved and then cast in resin. A small replica of the golden lion, a British symbol, is displayed on top.

15

16

17

15 In the French room, purple is used to symbolize royalty, emphasizing Napoleon's former role as Emperor.

16 17 This figure of Napoleon, together with its pull-out book showing views of Malmaison, was a chance find in our local antiques market. Black with age, both proved to be of silver when cleaned up; the book concealed within its silver cover is in perfect condition. These truly museum-quality exhibits are now displayed on the gilded eagle table in the Napoleonic room.

The samurai presence

The attic floor is reserved for my Japanese samurai warrior models. I became interested through studying samurai armour in museum collections and seeing it worn in action in films. Looked at close up the armour is beautiful and the workmanship exquisite. My models show a face, unlike some I have seen, where the helmet is designed not only for protection but to terrify the enemy – or the museum viewer.

18. The green wallpaper was chosen to give an impression of figures approaching through a forest, while cherry blossom, the symbol of the samurai, shimmers in the background.

19 20. Painted by a professional, the detail on the samurai's armour is exquisitely realistic.

Whether you actually have a warlike nature or not, there is no doubting the fascination of these finely detailed models to any miniaturist who looks at them closely. There are several different scales to choose from, all of which would be suitable for display in a 1:12 setting that may also include some furniture.

21. These 1:12 samurai swords on a traditional stand were made by a Japanese miniaturist, but bought at a miniatures fair in England. The stand-holder warned me to take care as the blades, here safely within their scabbards, are razor-sharp.

22 There are only a few parts to assemble, but this kit needs skilful painting to complete it. Horses are more difficult to paint successfully than uniforms, and using artists' oil paint rather than acrylic will give a better effect.

23 Wellington is mounted on his favourite horse, Copenhagen, in this splendid model. Wooden plinths are an optional addition that will give extra importance to completed figures. They are available in a choice of woods and a range of sizes from military model shops.

Military model kits

Painting the splendid uniforms and weapons can be an enjoyable challenge, but first you will need to assemble your chosen figure from a white-metal kit. You will find a wide selection in military model shops or by mail order.

The makers of good-quality cast metal kits generally provide instructions for initial preparation, together with a little advice on painting and the colours to be used, but are strangely silent as to how, exactly, to assemble the kit.

In the best kits, the parts arrive neatly laid out in a box in protective packaging; smaller kits can be just a pile of tiny pieces in a small pack. But a little common sense and careful sorting of the parts will give you some clues.

I have chosen two kits to feature: one of Wellington on horseback and one of Napoleon just after his abdication at Fontainebleau in 1814.

Here is some guidance to help you to achieve a spectacular figure.

Method

1 Clean the white-metal pieces carefully with steel wool; use a file and a craft knife to scrape off all mould lines in order to provide an even surface for painting.

2 Use a toothbrush to wash all parts with soap and water. This will remove any traces of oils.

3 Fill flaws with a filling paste and/or a two-component epoxy resin filler.

24 Napoleon at Fontainebleau about to sign his abdication. The parts to assemble this kit, made in Spain, are shown in their original packing. The ensemble includes a table on which to place the sword and epaulettes.

4 Assemble the figure using superglue or the type of model adhesive where two substances have to be mixed together before application. Check the parts and leave some to paint before gluing in place later. (Caution: see notes on using superglues on page 158.)

5 Apply a spray primer coat all over the figure. Primer for this purpose is available in white, grey or black.

6 Paint with acrylic paint, artists' oil paint, or model enamel. Using a fine brush and allow plenty of time for each colour to dry.

25 The realistic model was based on a painting of 1814 by Delaroche, at the time of Napoleon's first abdication. For the model painter, getting the facial features right is the key to success, and needs practice.

TIP

A better finish can be achieved by using black undercoat, even on faces, as the colours can be seen more clearly while painting.

Design a museum to house your special collection

This museum suits my particular, specialized miniatures collection, but its use in this manner is an idea that could be adapted to your own special interest. A shop on the ground floor with museum rooms above devoted to pottery, furniture or art would work equally well. Do some research in a real museum, before deciding on background papers and flooring, and choose furniture that will show off your collection to advantage. Then, when everything is arranged to your satisfaction, sit back and enjoy the displays.

Part three
Gardens and garden buildings

Chapter 12
Orangery and walled garden

Some gardeners are impatient and, instead of growing from seed, prefer to buy plants and cuttings that are already flourishing. For miniaturists who want to design a garden complete with a small building, a kit will provide, if not an instant garden, at least a short cut.

An orangery that can stand against the wall of a dolls' house, and a separate kit to make a walled garden that will surround it, is an imaginative idea. They can be used together, or either on its own will make an individual project.

Assembling an orangery kit

The kit I chose is made of plywood, and of such good quality that no initial sanding is necessary. To save you time and trouble, the glazing is already in place between the inner and outer window frames but has

not been not glued in – you can lift it out to paint the wood. Fine sandpaper is provided: you will need to use it if you smear a dab of paint on to the inside edge of a window or door frame, which would prevent the glazing fitting perfectly.

In this kit, the hinges are already fitted onto the doors and after painting, have only to be screwed on to the door frame.

Attention to detail has gone into this design; the instructions are clear, with coloured pictures showing

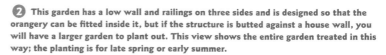

1 An orangery can be placed against a side wall of most dolls' houses; this example has no back, making it easy to lift away whenever you feel like changing the plants inside.

2 This garden has a low wall and railings on three sides and is designed so that the orangery can be fitted inside it, but if the structure is butted against a house wall, you will have a larger garden to plant out. This view shows the entire garden treated in this way; the planting is for late spring or early summer.

3 The orangery kit is well-presented, with clear instructions and coloured pictures to show each stage of assembly.

how the parts fit together at each stage. I don't think it would be possible to make a mistake!

To complete the orangery, you will need to provide your own choice of flooring. It can be of stone or brick cladding sheet, flagstones, or thick, rough card to simulate gravel. Textured card or coarse sandpaper can be painted with water-based paint to suggest whatever colour of gravelled surface you prefer.

The walled garden kit

Like the orangery, the walled garden is simple to assemble. The edges of the baseboard, the coping for the low wall and the pillars should be painted before assembly. A simulated stone will probably look best, and a textured stone paint looks realistic. The railings are made from plastic, not metal, and these can be painted rather than left black, if preferred.

4 Close to completion: it remains only to hinge on the doors and the final few window frames. The roof has been undercoated and sanded lightly before its final coat of paint.

5 The parts to make the walled garden are laid out on the base.

If you plan to attach your garden to a Georgian house, choose a dark green colour, as railings were not painted black until later in the 19th century.

Plan out your garden

The plants and flowers to go inside the orangery can be changed whenever you want, but you will need to plan a layout for the garden. Measure the space and cut a piece of thin card to this size. Draw out where you want paths or borders and choose where to place garden furniture or statuary. You might want a lawn or a paved area, or both.

Make a lawn and paths

Use railway modellers' fake lawn grass, which comes in a large sheet or roll that can be cut with scissors. If you want paths, these must be laid out first. Cut out the lawn pieces to

6 The partly assembled kit; before fitting in place the low wall has been covered with stone paper.

7 The holes to take the railings are ready-drilled, making it easy to glue them in place.

suit your design, and set them aside while you lay the paths. A quick and easy way to make gravel paths is to cut them from a medium sandpaper, which is already a suitable colour to simulate sandy gravel.

9 Daffodils herald spring, and bulbs are sprouting.

8 Spring: inside the orangery, flowers are almost ready to plant out.

⑩ Summer: the view from the orangery into the garden. There are now more flowers, while plants in containers add colour inside.

⑪ Summer is the time for sitting out; a rustic bench and a basket chair are ready for lazy afternoons. A border of deep pink flowers replaces the green of the hedge earlier in the year.

⑫ Fallen leaves and a basket of apples on the lawn look suitably autumnal. The leaves are turning on the potted shrubs too – these are small leafy twigs from my real garden. If you plan to change your garden scheme from time to time, you may find that, carefully chosen, small garden cuttings may come in useful to produce an instant effect at no cost.

Seasonal plantings

I soon found that I enjoyed miniature gardening so much that I designed some seasonal plantings, to vary the appearance of both orangery and garden at different times of the year. The schemes are realistic: in winter, plants inside the orangery are sheltered from frost in the garden; while in summer all the flowers are bursting into bloom. You can of course adapt these ideas to suit your own schemes.

TIP

Autumn is my favourite time of the year, and as I made this garden in October, I was able to make use of russet-coloured fallen leaves to scrunch up and scatter. A similar effect can be achieved with scraps of brown paper.

⑬ For a really chilly winter effect, I changed the lawn to paving, provided a formal hedge (made from cut-up green pan-cleaners) and added conifers.

Chapter 13
Greenhouse

For miniaturists who have only limited space available for a garden building, a greenhouse might be just what you need. This kit is quick to assemble, so you that can concentrate on choosing and arranging the flowers inside.

① The completed greenhouse, filled with colourful plants and flowers.

② This kit is a simple flat-pack assembly, making it straightforward to put together.

③ The shell is completed before the hinged roof is added.

This inexpensive kit is ready-painted and fitted with glazing. The roof hinges are already screwed in place on one side, and there are holes bored in the main roof beam for you to screw in the other side of the hinges. Brass screws are provided, but you will need a cross-headed screwdriver of the correct size.

If you do not have one already, these are inexpensive and will be a useful addition to your tool chest.

The kit assembly

There are no written instructions – a page of drawings identifies each part, with shaded areas that indicate

where to fit the parts together. It took me 15 minutes to unpack the pieces and check out what to do. After a cup of coffee, I assembled the greenhouse in 30 minutes.

Arranging the greenhouse

Some staging for potted plants is essential in a greenhouse. Simple staging is easy to make, using any

off-cuts of wood you have to hand. It can be quite roughly finished, as though the gardener had decided to knock something up quickly.

Method

1 Use ½in square (12mm) dowel and cut four pieces each 4in (100mm) long. Glue three of the lengths together, side by side.

2 Cut two pieces of dowel, each 1½in (38mm) long for supports.

4 Finials are provided to glue into pre-drilled holes in the roof ridging.

5 A neat example of ready-made staging, to hold plant pots and garden tools.

3 Glue the supports underneath, ½in (12mm) from each end.

4 Glue the fourth length on top of the back strip.

6 A few pieces of dowel are all you need to make simple staging.

7 The finished staging, which is left unpainted to show off these colourful flowers and packets of seeds.

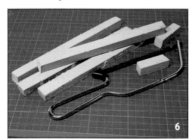

8 Both sets of staging find a place in the greenhouse.

Chapter 14
Garden furniture

Here is a range of outdoor furniture: how to assemble a bench from a kit; how to make a rustic garden bench and how to paint a gazebo. All will find a place in the miniaturist's garden.

This seat was designed by Sir Edwin Lutyens during his long collaboration with the Victorian gardener Gertrude Jekyll. It has become a classic and copies are still made today.

Assembling the kit

The Lutyens seat is available fully finished or to assemble from a kit made from MDF, cherry wood or spruce. I chose the cherry wood version.

This kit is laser-cut, an efficient way for a maker to duplicate intricate parts. The disadvantage is that on wood that is to be polished or varnished, a laser leaves scorch marks along all the cut edges, and these need to be sanded off to achieve an even colour. This is necessary only if you want a natural wood finish; in the MDF version, paint will cover the discolouration.

Sanding off the scorch marks is not for the faint-hearted, as it is a lengthy process. An ordinary 'diamond' nail file works better than sandpaper, and is also easy

① The completed Lutyens seat would add a touch of class to any garden or conservatory.

② The pre-cut parts ready to remove from the remaining wood.

③ Work in progress: the seat, the arm supports and the lower rails are glued into the front section after thorough sanding.

④ An emery board is useful but a diamond nail file makes sanding in between narrow spaces much easier.

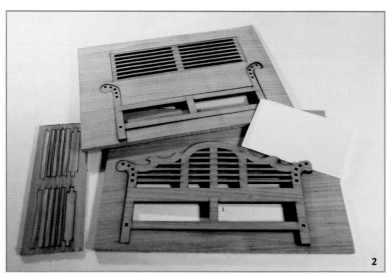

to get between the bars of the seat and back. You will need patience to remove all the scorching, but it will be worth the effort involved.

Method

1 Glue the main pieces together with wood adhesive, and tape with masking tape until the glue is set.

2 Dry fit the arm supports and lower rails into the mortise holes on the front and back. To ensure a perfect fit, sand the ends of the supports and rails carefully, on both front and back, before you glue them in place.

3 The mortise joints are meant to show, as this is Arts & Crafts furniture, but it is worth spending time to make them perfect.

4 Rub over with finishing paper, and then with a good-quality wax polish. Don't over-polish – remember this is a garden seat and not for indoor use.

A rustic garden bench

If you want to build something for your garden from 'found' materials without any expense, you might like to try making a rustic-style bench from twigs.

Method

1 Collect twigs from a garden, making sure that they are not too dried out, or rotten through damp. A dry day at the end of summer is the best time to search.

2 Draw out the design you want, and measure carefully, as you do not want a lopsided bench. It needs to look as though it could be sat on without collapsing. Cut the twigs to length with a fine saw blade to make neat ends.

3 After that, all you need is a bit of patience and all-purpose glue to fix the twigs together. To preserve the completed bench, finish it with a coat of matt varnish.

Paint a gazebo

Chinese 1:12 garden furniture made from wire is widely available. It is always supplied in a white finish, but looks even better if you spray-paint it in a soft green.

Method

1 Use a paint developed for miniaturist/hobby use, not car spray paint, which is thick and liable to clog the wire mesh.

2 Work outdoors or in a well-ventilated room. Put the miniature inside a large cardboard box and

make sure that you cover the surrounding area with sheets of newspaper.

3 Spray gently and evenly and leave to dry thoroughly before handling. To move the miniature to spray all sides, pick it up and change position with two cocktail sticks.

4 If any holes in the wire mesh are partly filled with paint, pierce them gently with a pin and check that each side is clear.

6 A gazebo will suit any style of garden – here one is shown on a roof garden.

Chapter 15
Conservatory

Gardening can be hard work, although always enjoyable. Similarly, after completing all the gardening projects in this section, I want to show an example of a garden building that is ready-built and decorated, so that you can begin on arranging the plants and flowers in it immediately.

① A beautifully finished conservatory, with a paved floor, stained-glass insets and double doors with working bolts and latches to keep them safely closed when not in use.

A fully finished conservatory is naturally the most expensive option but is sure to provide hours of pleasure. My example, made by a miniaturist who never makes two exactly alike, will give the added satisfaction to any hobbyist of knowing that it is unique.

A conservatory similar to this one can be used to extend the boundaries of the dolls' house; it is large enough to use as a kitchen extension, a children's playroom or a summer dining room. Or, as shown, a place to sit and relax.

Arranging your conservatory

Put your own personal stamp on your conservatory – there are limitless ways to arrange it. The practical gardener may choose to show it in use, like the scheme pictured opposite, with bulbs ready to plant, gardening tools and plant pots. Or it can be used for leisure, with a table laid for tea as a centrepiece and a chair to recline in. You may want to train climbing plants against the window frames or across the glass roof, fill urns and decorative containers with prize

② A stork perched on top brings it all to life.

specimens or include ferns and foliage to make a green haven. You could include a fountain or a statue as a focal point, make a Lutyens garden seat from a kit (shown on page 150), spray paint wire chairs, a table or an *étagère*, or add a flower basket filled with 'freshly picked' roses.

TIP

If you are neat fingered and enjoy working in very small scale, you can make your own flowers from a huge range of tiny kits available by mail order or at dolls' house shops.

③ The inside of this conservatory was arranged by a hobbyist who is also a passionate gardener.

④ Sculpture looks its best amidst greenery. This cherub is painted to resemble an old lead statue.

⑤ A fountain is just as suitable inside a conservatory as in a garden courtyard.

⑥ ⑦ Humble lavender or a prize specimen – choose your favourite plants to make your conservatory special.

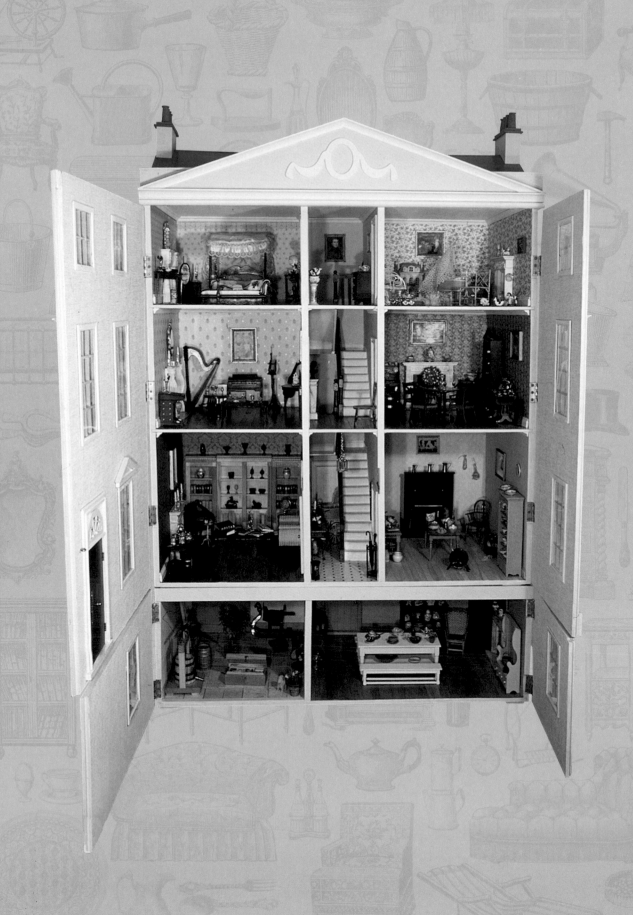

Part four
Practical advice

Tools and techniques

This book covers a wide range of styles, the decoration of ready-made dolls' houses and kit assemblies of others. Each project covers the process in detail, but this section provides additional guidance that will be useful to a beginner and serves as a reminder to the more experienced.

There is a step-by-step assembly of a house kit suitable for a beginner, a list of the tools and materials you will need, and two furniture kits to make up, covering the whole process from unpacking the parts to how to complete the finishing. There is also a reference table of suitable exterior and interior decorative finishes and colours to suit dolls' houses of each featured period.

Tools

These simple tools can be obtained from suppliers of art materials, good stationers or craft shops, and dolls' house shops that cater for the hands-on miniaturist.

Self-healing cutting mat
Buy one marked with a squared grid.

Craft knife with replaceable blades
If you are unsure how to change the blades, ask for a demonstration.

Transparent 18in (460mm) ruler
This is helpful when measuring out wallpaper to match a pattern.

Metal ruler with raised edge
Use as a cutting guide. It is worth paying a little more for a thick ruler designed for professional use, rather than a cheap, flimsy one.

Screwdrivers
You will need one very small screwdriver and a selection of cross-headed screwdrivers to suit different sizes of screw heads.

Junior hacksaw
Use to cut metal, plastic and wood.

Metal mini mitre box
Use this with a fine saw blade fitted into a handle, so that the saw blade can be changed when it becomes worn. It is useful for cutting mitres on wooden mouldings.

Mini electric drill
Not essential but very useful to fit door knobs and to pre-drill holes for screws.

❶ Basic tools for the miniaturist, laid out on the essential cutting mat.

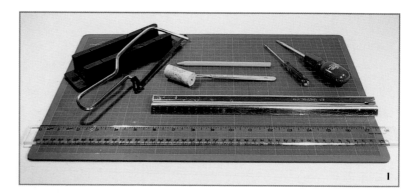

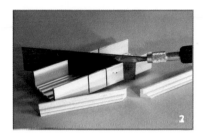

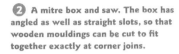

2 A mitre box and saw. The box has angled as well as straight slots, so that wooden mouldings can be cut to fit together exactly at corner joins.

3 4 Skirting cut at an angle to make a neat join at a corner. Cutting a mitre requires practice, but with the aid of the box a perfect join can be achieved.

Useful materials

Masking tape
Use to hold small parts together while glue sets. Also use it to make clean, straight lines when paints of different colours are used next to each other.

Parcel tape
Use for taping pieces together while glue sets, e.g. the walls and floor, or roof of a dolls' house built from a kit.

Acetate sheet
For dolls' house window glazing, this is available in A4 sheets and there are different thicknesses. Choose one that is not too thick to cut easily but not so thin that it bends and flexes.

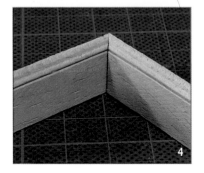

Double-sided adhesive tape
Use to attach flooring; this is preferable to gluing it in place as it will then be easy to remove it if you decide on a change at a later date.

Thin cardboard
Use to cut a template so that wooden or plasticized sheet flooring can be glued onto this as a base, before fixing to the dolls' house floor.

Wooden mouldings
For skirting boards, cornice and dado rails. A wide range of patterns is available to suit different period styles. It is also worth checking out the hardware store for narrow mouldings intended as edging strip.

Balsa wood
This is available in several thicknesses. It is useful for making chimney breasts, provided they are covered with cladding, as it does not take paint or varnish well.

5 Fitting a door knob is simple with a mini electric drill.

6 Masking tape and parcel tape are invaluable for use while glue sets. Sandpaper in several grades is another essential.

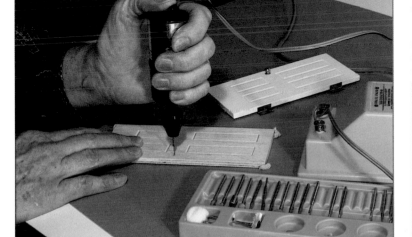

Adhesives

For the main projects in this book, you will only need one adhesive – PVA wood adhesive. This provides permanent fixing of wood: once set, the bond cannot be undone. It can be squeezed straight from the tube or container on to one surface only and spread evenly with a plastic spreader. Press the parts to be joined together – any excess adhesive must be wiped off immediately with a damp cloth. Large parts can be taped together with parcel tape for a few hours while glue sets before the next stage of assembly.

Similarly, when making up furniture from kits, take your time and do not try to add another part before the adhesive has set firmly. It may seem tempting, but you might end up with a lopsided piece if you are impatient.

All-purpose glue
This can be useful for attaching very small parts together, and for fixing wooden mouldings such as cornice and dado rails and skirtings that may need to be taken out for redecoration at a later date.

Impact or superglue
This is used to fix metal parts together and to glue metal to wood – for example, furniture castors to wooden legs.

7 This kit house is made from MDF and the parts are ready-painted both outside and in. The delicate pale blue with white trim reminds me of Regency seaside houses, which were painted in pastel colours.

> **TIP**
>
> Take care when using superglue, to avoid getting it on fingers and then even worse, transferring it to your face. It sticks skin together. Read the maker's instructions thoroughly and wash any spot off straight away with water and detergent. Avoid eye contact, which is dangerous. One useful method is to apply it with a plastic cocktail stick.

Build a dolls' house from a kit

Building from a kit is always a cheaper option than buying ready-made; it is interesting and enjoyable and you will have a great sense of achievement from completing your very own dolls' house.

It is essential to choose your kit carefully and make sure that it will be within your capabilities. Some are simple enough for a beginner, others will need some experience, while a few are for those with a working knowledge of woodwork techniques, professional tools and a workshop. I have made up all the featured kits

and given comprehensive guides to assembly for each type, with pictures of work in progress at different stages. You may not have an identical kit, but the advice and help given with these examples will be invaluable when you come to tackle a kit yourself.

Choosing your kit

A beginner will have no problems with a simple two-room house of MDF (medium density fibreboard) but a larger and more complex house with perhaps ten rooms, porticoes

and a staircase with landings, is best tackled when you have mastered basic methods and techniques. It is a good idea to make up a small house before you tackle something larger.

No keen miniaturist can ever have too many dolls' houses, and a design that will be equally attractive to children or grandchildren can be passed on if you decide to assemble a house with more rooms in the future.

With this in mind, here is an example of an inexpensive house that can be tackled with confidence by a beginner. I have provided a step-by-step guide with pictures of each stage of assembly. The house has accurate architectural details, and three good-sized rooms plus an attic and a staircase. It is ready-painted and could be furnished appropriately by a new hobbyist on a limited budget or by a collector of fine furniture.

The kit assembly

1 Begin by checking over all the parts to familiarize yourself with how they will fit together. To make the process easier, the instructions are given in a checklist.

2 Glue the ready-glazed window frames on to the façade. When the glue has set, glue the inner window frames in place. To complete the façade, glue on the front door and its surround. A brass door knob is provided and the hole for it has been pre-drilled.

8 The kit is well packed, with each part separately wrapped. There are a lot of parts, but only five are needed to complete the shell and two to make the roof.

9 One window frame is in place and the other remains to be glued on.

3 Screw together the side walls and the base. If you wish, you can use glue as well, but it seems unnecessary. I found it easier to lay the house on its back while fixing the screws. Although this kit is of MDF, it is not excessively heavy and is therefore easy to handle. Next screw on the back roof section.

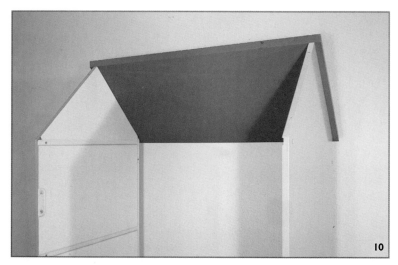

4 Add the front roof section. Note: take care to fit the roof sections the right way up! This is the only time I had a moment's hesitation. Look at the picture provided with the kit carefully, and it will soon become obvious. Then slide the back into position and screw it in place.

5 Slide the floors into the pre-cut grooves and secure them in place using screws.

6 Hinge on the front – the hinges are of the cranked type that are easy to deal with, even if you have never fitted hinges before. The usual snag in fitting hinges is the difficulty of getting each side accurately in the right place – no such problem here, as the holes are ready drilled to take the screws. Lay the house on its side and put a piece of wood under the

10 The shell is assembled and the back section of roof screwed on.

11 Both sections of roof are in place and the back can now be slid in and screwed on.

12 The floors slide into the pre-cut grooves.

13

14

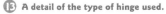

⑬ A detail of the type of hinge used.

⑭ The ready-assembled cupboard that fits under the staircase is beautifully finished and has shelves inside.

⑮ The house is complete and ready to furnish.

15

front so that it is on the same level as the shell. It will also help to keep it steady while you fit the screws.

7 To assemble the staircase, glue the round peg at the base of each baluster into the drilled holes. Check the fit, and if necessary sand down the peg slightly.

8 Glue in the understairs cupboard, the staircase and the landings. Then finally, glue the screw-covers over the screws on the outside walls and roof and add the chimneys and the magnetic catches.

I have gone into some detail on this assembly as an example of a dolls' house that can be made from a kit without any problems – no fuss, no mess, no need for painting. It should give you the confidence to tackle a more complex kit later on.

General hints on kit assembly

Instructions for kit assembly can vary a great deal, as each dolls' house designer has chosen their own method. It is vital to take the time to read through the instructions or check out the drawings that sometimes take the place of written guidance, to make absolutely sure that you understand what you are going to do before you begin.

• MDF kits usually have pre-cut grooves to fit parts into. Glue alone may be sufficient but some kits provide screws (and pre-drilled holes) for extra strength.

• Plywood kits need panel pins as well as glue. It is important that pins are driven in straight and not at an angle, through both sections to be joined. Draw a pencil line on the outside of a panel to correspond with the centre of any rebate on the reverse side before you tap in the panel pins.

• Do *not* use clamps unless you have woodwork experience, as they could cause distortion. Parts are best held together with parcel tape or masking tape while glue sets. Check corners are square using a set square.

• Hinging on fronts can be a problem for the inexperienced. The easiest type of hinge to fit is the cranked hinge, which has largely superseded earlier types of hinge.

Lay the front-opening façade flat, about ¼in (6mm) away from the front of the side wall of the assembled carcass, and support both on a piece of wood to raise them to a level height above the workbench or table – about 1in (25mm) is sufficient. This will allow the knuckle of the hinge to sit properly in the small gap between the two.

Remember to allow clearance so that when hinged on, the front, when opened inwards, will not scrape along the inside floor of the house. The façade should lie about ¼in (6mm) higher than the floor level inside the house – but check the thickness of the flooring you intend to use with care.

Makers are aware of this potential problem, and many kit houses now have pre-drilled screw holes.

Extend your dolls' house with extra rooms

Whether you have a ready-made dolls' house or one that you have made up from a kit, many makers can provide a basement as an optional addition. A basement must be designed to fit the model that you have.

Adding a basement means that there must be some sort of entrance below the main house: either a pavement with an area underneath, or some entrance steps that can be lifted off to open up the basement. Each maker will have designed their own ingenious solution, but measure your display area carefully before you decide on this addition. It will extend the depth of your dolls' house so that it may no longer fit on the table or cupboard on which you planned it should stand.

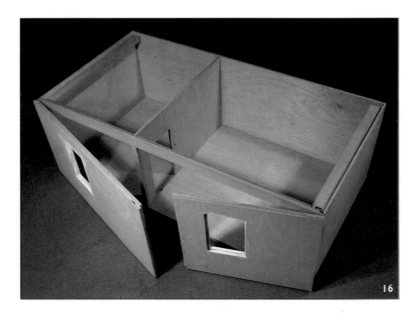

16 An example of a two-room basement that is simple to assemble. In this case, rebates at back and sides are designed so that the main house sits neatly on top.

Decoration guide

Exterior decoration Suitable colours and exterior finishes for houses of different periods

Period	Finishes	
Early Tudor (late 15th–early 16th century)	Walls	Plaster with half timbering. Off-white, ochre, grey infill.
	Timbers	Paint as weathered old oak using grey-white mix or use wood stain, light or medium oak.
	Roof	Stone tiles or simulated thatch.
	Front door	Oak with ring handle and iron hinges.
Mid–late Tudor (mid–late 16th century)	Walls	Plaster with half timbering. Off-white, ochre, pale pink, terracotta or apricot infill, or brick infill.
	Timbers	Light or medium oak wood stain. Use walnut wood stain to give a warmer appearance.
	Roof	Stone tiles or grey or russet slate.
	Front door	As early Tudor.
Classical Georgian (18th–early 19th century)	Walls	Paint as stone for a town or country house. Satin finish gives a good effect.
	Roof	Grey slates or grey paint.
	Paintwork	'Georgian' white – off-white – for window frames and surrounds.
	Front door	Dark green, black or white.
	Railings	Today's Georgian house has black-painted railings, but a dark bronze-green is historically correct.
Regency Gothic (late 18th–early 19th century)	Walls	Paint as stucco: grey or terracotta matt finish or textured.
	Roof	Grey slate or paint. Paint architectural mouldings as stone: use matt finish model enamel.
	Front door	Stain as oak or paint white. Add lanterns on either side.

French farmhouse or manor house		
	Walls	Matt paint. Pink, off-white, apricot, terracotta or stone.
	Shutters	Pale or mid-blue, white, deep red.
	Roof	Grey slate or paint; russet tiles in some areas of France.
	Paintwork	White or greenish-blue, any shade of blue.
	Front door	White or stain as oak.
Dutch house (17th century)	Walls	Brick with stone trim or stucco painted as stone.
	Shutters	Red or mid-green.
	Roof	Grey.
	Paintwork	Off-white or blue-grey.
	Front door	As paintwork.

Interior decoration Suitable colours and finishes for interiors of different periods

Period	Finishes	
Early Tudor (late 15th–early 16th century)	Walls	Off-white, terracotta matt finish paint.
	Ceilings	Off-white; distressed oak beams can be added.
	Floors	Beaten earth (paint as earth), stone, uneven flagstones, planked (wide oak floorboards).
Mid–late Tudor (mid–late 16th century)	Walls	As early Tudor; beams may be painted in red or green with a decorative design.
	Ceilings	Plasterwork, sometimes elaborate.
	Floors	Stone or planked, as early Tudor.
	Additions	Wall panelling; inglenook fireplaces.

Classical Georgian (18th–early 19th century)	Walls	Off-white matt paint in service rooms. Wallpapers in best rooms, or matt paint in 'Adam' green. Panelling, painted mid-green, is an option.
	Ceilings	Off-white.
	Floors	Oak planks, unpolished, or pine in service rooms.
	Additions	Skirting board, cornice and dado rail, painted off-white. Plain marble fireplaces, hob grates in small rooms.
Late Georgian/early Victorian (early–mid-19th century)	Walls	More elaborate wallpapers, sometimes flocked.
	Ceilings	Plasterwork with painted decoration, sometimes gilded.
	Floors	Planked and polished, partly covered with patterned or needlepoint carpets.
	Additions	Elaborate curtains, blinds, ceiling roses and crystal chandeliers.
		Elaborate marble fireplaces with brass fenders.
Regency Gothic (late 18th–early 19th century)	Walls	Wallpapers in deep, rich colours; pink for picture or sculpture gallery (matt paint).
	Ceilings	Plasterwork imitating medieval style. Elaborate ceiling roses.
	Floors	Marble, granite or stone.
	Additions	Plasterwork frieze, gilded cornice; skirtings can be stone. Elaborate curtains. Gothic fireplaces.
Arts & Crafts style (late 19th–early 20th century)	Walls	Plain cream, or William Morris wallpaper.
	Ceilings	Cream or off-white.
	Floors	Oak planks with rugs or a carpet square and polished surround or flagstones.
	Additions	Oak picture rail or plate rack.

French farmhouse

	Walls	Plaster; simulate with plain textured wallpaper. Cream or stone colour, or terracotta.
	Ceilings	Off-white; distressed beams painted grey-white (optional).
	Floors	Tiled, red and green, blue and white with border tiles (optional). Tiles can be lozenge-shaped or hexagonal. Planked in upper rooms and stained as walnut.
	Additions	French-style fireplaces.

French manor house

	Walls	Stone hall. Pretty wallpapers, *toile de Jouy* in best rooms, especially bedrooms.
	Ceilings	Off-white, beams are optional.
	Floors	Tiles as for farmhouse; marble; carpeted in some rooms.
	Additions	Large, impressive fireplaces. Fine furniture, sometimes gilded or painted.

Dutch house
(17th century)

	Walls	Cream or off-white.
	Ceilings	As above.
	Floors	Dutch tiles – black and white, red and green, ochre and brown, grey and black. Planked in upper rooms.
	Additions	Blue-and-white tiled skirtings (optional).

21st-century home

	Walls	Pale colours, paint or paper.
	Ceilings	White.
	Floors	Use textured wallpaper to simulate tiled floor or carpet.
	Additions	Spiral staircase painted as metal. Roof garden.

Furniture for your dolls' house

Examples of beautiful, professionally made furniture are shown in the dolls' houses featured throughout this book. The pictured rooms also include painted furniture – which are either whitewood or inexpensive pieces given a new finish – and furniture assembled from kits.

Painted furniture

Painted furniture is often included in schemes by professional interior decorators; why not follow their example and paint your own? Whitewood furniture is generally well made and inexpensive. After the wood has been given a light sanding, an acrylic paint will work well.

Furniture to assemble from kits

Furniture kits are economical and fun to assemble. Provided care is taken with the finishing, you will have a piece of furniture of which you can be proud. The pieces that I chose to suit the period style of each featured house fit in well with other furniture in the rooms.

Two useful pieces to assemble from kits – a dressing table and a child's bed – provide a demonstration of how to make up and finish a kit successfully. The following points apply to these or similar kits.

• Check the parts and read the instructions carefully – twice!

17

17 A settle used in my Georgian house servants' hall, painted with acrylic paint in a soft green.

18 For the long table and benches in the same room, I chose a creamy white, to give a well-scrubbed look. The side pieces and legs are darkened slightly with a blue glaze.

18

- Gently sand all parts using a fine sandpaper.

- Be careful to wipe off any excess glue with a damp cloth or damp cotton bud, as any traces left behind will spoil the finish.

- Careful finishing is the key to success, and it is worth taking time at this stage. It can be varnished, with satin varnish, or polished.

- To polish, use 00 grade wire wool and apply a good-quality wax polish to all surfaces. Buff to a shine with a soft cloth. Repeat waxing until the desired depth of polish is achieved.

19 There are only nine pieces to be joined to make this dressing table.

20 The legs are glued to the side and end pieces and the top is ready to fit.

21 The top is fitted with the routed edge at the front and the plain edge at the back: the dressing table is now complete.

22

All wood darkens gradually; if you want to add furniture to a room containing pieces that you have had for some time, you may find that choosing the same wood for your miniature is not enough to prevent it looking lighter in colour. To darken the wood more quickly, apply a thin coat of boiled linseed oil with a paintbrush and wipe off the excess with a soft cloth. Leave to dry for 12 hours, before polishing.

Note that furniture kits made of whitewood will need staining before polishing. Alternatively, try a painted finish, which often looks better on whitewood and, if it is a period-style piece, it can be gently aged after painting with a little smudged-on acrylic paint.

23

22 The parts to make the child's bed are sorted out. Glue the tall posts to the headboard and the short ones to the footboard. Then add the sides.

23 Glue the slats into the grooved inner side edges of the bed.

24 To finish the bed, the top edges of the headboard and footboard must be gently sanded to round them off.

24

Makers of featured miniatures

In a book with so many wide-ranging projects, it is impossible to credit every single miniaturist. This list mentions the makers of items shown in the photographs. For more information on professional miniaturists, look in the advertisement pages of dolls' house magazines or see miniatures fair programmes.

Suppliers

Dolls' houses and miniatures:

Barbara's Mouldings
tel/fax: +44(0) 1572 770383
email:
orders@barbarasmouldings.com
(Colour catalogue)

Blackwells of Hawkwell
tel: +44(0) 1702 200036
fax: +44(0) 1702 204211
email:
sales@blackwells-miniatures.com
www.blackwells-miniatures.com
(Colour catalogue)

Borcraft Miniatures
tel/fax: +44(0) 1964 537722
email: @borcraft-miniatures.co.uk
www.borcraft-miniatures.co.uk
(Catalogue)

Classic Carpets (Germany)
tel: 0049 40491 7274
fax: 0049 40412 85165
email: sybylle.dawson@hamburg.de

The Dolls' House Emporium
Freephone: 0800 0523 643
fax: +44(0) 1773 513772
www.dollshouse.com
(Free colour catalogue)

Glenowen Ltd
tel/fax: +44(0) 116240 4373
email: chris@glenowen.fsnet.co.uk
www.glenowendhf.co.uk
(Colour catalogue)

Jackson's Miniatures Ltd
tel: +44(0) 1747 824851
fax: +44(0) 1747 824105
www.jacksonsminiatures.com
(Catalogue)

Robert Longstaff Workshops
tel: +44(0)1865 820206
fax: +44(0) 1865 821089
www.longstaff.co.uk

McQueenie Miniatures
tel: +44(0) 1493 780140
email: b.mcq@btinternet.com
www.btinternet.com/-b.mcq
(Catalogue)

Maple Street Miniatures
tel: +44(0) 1223 207025/
208937
fax: +44(0) 1223 207021
www.maplestreet.co.uk
(Free colour catalogue)

Margaret's Miniatures
tel: +44(0) 1985 846797
fax: +44(0) 1985 846796
(Colour catalogue)

The Original Dolls House Company
tel: +44(0) 1435 864155
fax: +44(0) 1435 865108
www.dijon.co.uk
(Colour catalogue)

Pulteney Bridge Gifts of Bath
tel/fax: +44(0) 1225 426161
www.dollshouseminiaturesofbath.co.uk

Sid Cooke Dolls' Houses
tel: +44(0) 1922 633422
fax: +44(0) 1922 650240
www.sidcooke.com
(Colour catalogue)

Tollgate Miniatures and Small Interiors (France)
tel/fax: 0033 233 30 49 39
email:
tollgateminiatures@hotmail.com
www.tollgateminiatures.co.uk
(Catalogue)

Military model kits:

Andrea Miniatures (Spain)
tel: (34) 91 857 00 08
fax: (34) 91 857 00 48
email: andrea@ctv.es
www.andrea-miniatures.com

Bonapartes
tel/fax: +44(0) 1225 423873
www.bonapartes.co.uk

Bibliography

Coignard, Jérôme
Provence Style of Living
Hachette ill./Octopus 2002

Collard, Frances
Regency Furniture
Antique Collector's Club 1985

Conran, Terence
Small Spaces
Conran Octopus 2001

Dickson, Elizabeth (Editor)
The English Garden Room
Weidenfeld & Nicolson 1986 paperback

Evans, Tony & Lycett Green, Candida
English Cottages
Weidenfeld & Nicolson 1982 paperback

Fiske, John & Freeman, Lisa
Living with Early Oak
The Belmont Press 2005

Forgeur, Brigitte
Living in Amsterdam
Thames & Hudson (via Amazon)

Foxton, Howard
Shakespeure Country
Grange Books 1995

Hendy, Jenny
Zen in Your Garden
Godsfield Press 2001

Marston, Peter
The Conservatory Book
Cassell 2001

Michels, Heide
Monet's House: An Impressionist Interior
Frances Lincoln 1997

Parissien, Steven
The Georgian Group Book of The Georgian House
Aurum Press 1995

Parissien, Steven
Regency Style
Phaidon 1992

Percival, Joyce
Architecture for Dolls' Houses
GMC Publications

Prizeman, John
Your House the Outside View
Quiller Press 1982 (recently reissued in paperback)

Roberts, Andrew
Napoleon & Wellington
Weidenfeld & Nicolson 2001, paperback 2003

Saudan-Skira, Sylvia & Saudan, Michel
Orangeries: Palaces of Glass – their history and development
Taschen 1998

Spencer-Churchill, Henrietta
Classic English Interiors
Collins & Brown 1990, paperback 2001

Spencer-Churchill, Henrietta
Classic Georgian Style
Collins & Brown 1997, paperback 2001

Stoeltie, Barbara & René
Country Houses of France
Taschen 1999

Thorneycroft, Johanna & Von Einsiedel, Andreas
The Provencal House
Scriptum Editions 2003

Walshe, Paul & Miller, John
French Farmhouses & Cottages
Weidenfeld & Nicolson 1992 paperback

Acknowledgements

My thanks are due to everyone involved with the production of this book – to Gerrie Purcell for her help and advice, to my editor Rachel Netherwood for her enthusiasm and efficiency, and to designer Chloë Alexander.

I am grateful to my local dolls' house shops, Caroline Nevill Miniatures of Bath, Pulteney Bridge Gifts of Bath and Margaret's Miniatures of Warminster, for loaning miniatures for photography, and to Karon Butler and Cathy Creed, who were always available to deal with requests and find just what I needed.

Barbara's Mouldings, The Dolls' House Emporium, Glenowen Ltd, Jackson's Miniatures Ltd, Sid Cooke Dolls' Houses and Tollgate Miniatures were generous in supplying kits for me to build and decorate, while furniture kits were kindly supplied by Blackwells of Hawkwell (for Mini Mundus),

Robert Longstaff Workshops and McQueenie Miniatures. Bonapartes of Bath loaned military models for our photography; I would like to acknowledge the skills of David Freeman, who painted most of the models in my own collection, and of Bruce Stuart, who painted the samurai warrior figure.

And a big thank you to June Wright, friend, hobbyist and collector, who was always ready to provide a second pair of hands, to assemble furniture kits and to paint furniture, and even on one occasion to stain 130 pieces of wood moulding without complaint.

This, my tenth book, is a tribute to all the miniaturists who have become my friends over the years.

For me it is also a special book, because my husband Alec, who has devoted so much of his time to photographing dolls' houses and miniatures and work in progress for me for my previous books, on this occasion has taken all the photographs.

About the author

Jean Nisbett began to take notice of period houses, their decorations and furniture before she was ten years old, and they have been a major interest ever since. While bringing up a family, she began working in miniature scale and has since developed an equal enthusiasm for reproducing modern architecture and design small scale. Her work has been shown on the BBC, Channel 4, UK Style and TF1 France.

She began writing while working in the London offices of an American advertising agency and is well-known as the leading British writer on dolls' houses and miniatures. Her articles have appeared in specialist dolls' house magazines since 1985, and regularly in GMC's *The Dolls' House Magazine* since the first issue in 1998.

Jean lives in Somerset, south-west England, and this is her tenth book for GMC Publications.

Index

To place an order, or to request a catalogue, contact:
GMC Publications
Castle Place, 166 High Street, Lewes, East Sussex, BN7 1XU United Kingdom
Tel: 01273 488005 Fax: 01273 402866
Website: www.thegmcgroup.com
Orders by credit card are accepted